UP
YOUR
GAME!

Also by Gary Belsky and Neil Fine

ON THE ORIGINS OF SPORTS

*The Early History and Original Rules of
Everybody's Favorite Games*

23 WAYS TO GET TO FIRST BASE

The ESPN Uncyclopedia

ANSWER GUY

*Extinguishing the Burning Questions of Sports
with the Water Bucket of Truth*

UP
YOUR
GAME!

Skills, Tips, and Strategies to Achieve Total Sports Mastery

GARY BELSKY & NEIL FINE

ARTISAN | NEW YORK

Library of Congress Cataloging-in-Publication Data

Names: Belsky, Gary, author. | Fine, Neil, 1962- author.

Title: Up your game / Gary Belsky and Neil Fine.

Description: New York : Artisan Books, [2017] | Includes index.

Identifiers: LCCN 2016038088 | ISBN 9781579657406 (Paperback)

Subjects: LCSH: Sports—Handbooks, manuals, etc.

Classification: LCC GV704 .B45 2017 | DDC 796—dc23 LC record available at https://lccn.loc.gov/2016038088

Cover and interior design and interior icons by Paul Kepple & Max Vandenberg at Headcase Design

Artisan books are available at special discounts when purchased in bulk for premiums and sales promotions as well as for fund-raising or educational use. Special editions or book excerpts also can be created to specification. For details, contact the Special Sales Director at the address below, or send an e-mail to specialmarkets@workman.com.

Published by Artisan

A division of Workman Publishing Co., Inc.

225 Varick Street

New York, NY 10014-4381

artisanbooks.com

Artisan is a registered trademark of Workman Publishing Co., Inc.

Published simultaneously in Canada by Thomas Allen & Son, Limited

Printed in China

First printing, March 2017

10 9 8 7 6 5 4 3 2 1

To my siblings—
Rhona, Howard, Jonathan, and Barbara—
who raised my game.

—G. B.

To Mom and Dad, who showed me all the steps
but didn't force me to follow them.

—N. F.

CONTENTS

Sound Like You Know What You're Talking About: *Basketball Edition* 240

INTRODUCTION

A FUNNY THING HAPPENS when people learn that you are (or were) the editor in chief or executive editor at *ESPN The Magazine*. After they ask you to identify your most obnoxious on-air colleagues (there were none—all were fine Americans), folks start peppering you with a litany of questions. It is the non–potentially lifesaving version of the guy who hounds the doctor he just met at a party to diagnose various aches and pains. Some questions are of a trivial nature—say, which set of brothers holds the NHL record for most career goals? (Wayne and Brent Gretzky—but mostly Wayne.) Some pry for insider intel, like, is that player/team/coach/ GM as talented/evil/incompetent/brilliant as people say? (Probably—except when he/she/they are not.) Other questions demand a little more pondering, be they provocative (Who's the best football coach of all time?) or particular (How do they get broncos to buck like that?), practical (How do I become an agent?) or personal (Is it okay to propose at a baseball game?).

Of course, we never had all the answers. What we did have, though, was the means to get them. And here they are. *Up Your Game!* is a curated representation of a fair amount of accumulated experience: ours, but also that of dozens of professional athletes and experts who were kind enough to share their hard-earned wisdom. It is a compendium of what you might call "yokel knowledge"—the customs, codes, and unwritten rules of fandom— along with insights into the fundamental skills of the games we love. From snagging an autograph to fielding a ground ball, from nailing a high five to landing an Ollie, from bluffing in poker to betting in golf—the entries add up to a user's manual and field guide rolled into one. This doesn't mean you'll agree with everything in here, but that's sports. One fan's treasure is another's trash (talk).

This kind of wisdom generally accrues in random moments over years and years of playing or rooting. So this book is organized in a similarly unpredictable fashion. Much of the joy of sports, for athletes and fans alike, is in the journey, a path of discovery with surprises that pop up along the way. That's why you'll find an All-Pro wide receiver's advice for catching a football (useful to any weekend warrior) next to a recipe for the perfect mint julep (useful to any Kentucky Derby fan). The hundreds of nuggets in this book have a single mission—to enhance your experience as a fan or your efforts as an athlete. And when you're done reading it all, you too will have an easy answer to all the hard questions: Read the book!

—G. B. & N. F.

CATCH A FOUL BALL

It's like winning the lottery writ small, but unlike with the lottery, there are real ways to improve your chances of taking home a game-used memento of your night at the ballpark.

CHOOSE YOUR MATCHUP WISELY. Hard-throwing pitchers usually generate more fouls than junk ballers.

DON'T BRING A GLOVE. Unless you've yet to hit puberty. It will make you look a little . . . delicate. Even the hardest line drive shouldn't do serious damage to your hands.

FIND THE RIGHT SPOT. As a rule, most foul balls land in either the upper deck behind home plate or the lower deck down the baselines. Fields with more expansive foul territories mean fewer chances for a ball to reach the baseline stands, so in such cases, the upper deck behind home is the way to go. All things being equal, though, keep in mind that your odds of catching a ball increase if you're sitting in a sparsely populated section.

THINK AHEAD. To be in the right place at the right time, you need to know when the right time is. Keep an eye on the lineup: Contact hitters generally foul off more pitches than sluggers. You don't want to be in the bathroom when those guys are due to bat.

PLAY NICELY WITH OTHERS. The last thing you want is to wind up in a viral video for knocking some sweet old lady into the next row just to grab a souvenir. Carve out some suitable personal space and stick to it. Baseball gods reward the courteous. (Or if they don't, they should.)

WIN YOUR FANTASY LEAGUE

Fantasy sports were invented to let couch jockeys in on the action. And while the games are fake, winning them takes real effort. Here's how to compete without expending too much energy.

DO YOUR RESEARCH. Many inexperienced fantasy players view draft prep as a binary proposition: either you cram for days or it doesn't matter. Not so. In most leagues, a couple of hours of focused work is all it takes to be competitive. Print a cheat sheet (or two) from a reliable source and highlight whom the experts have identified as ready-to-break-out sleepers and ready-to-fade stars. You really don't need more than that.

DON'T LET YOUR HEART RULE YOUR HEAD. The fan in you hates a particular team or player. The fantasy owner in you needs to leave those biases to real life. If you want to win your league, scoring potential trumps personal vendetta. (We know—it's hard.)

TAKE A CHANCE. It's crazy to draft a possible breakout player six rounds earlier than cheat sheets project. It's genius to pull the trigger two (or three) rounds early.

FORGIVE FALLEN ANGELS. Is the 100th player on your cheat sheet still available as you contemplate pick 130? Give him strong consideration. Sure, he might be tainted for a reason. But one such roll of the dice per draft is worth the gamble. Sports, you might have heard, is about redemption.

MASTER THE MIX. Fantasy teams, like their real-life counterparts, need chemistry. Drafting too many players who could be either revelations or busts is a messy all-or-nothing proposition. Sometimes, the right call is a dependable, consistent asset whose ceiling may be low but whose basement door is locked.

REMEMBER YOUR STATS 101 CLASS. Early in the season, be on the lookout for other teams' struggling stars. There's a decent chance owners will give up on them for lesser players riding a hot start. And when they do, grab them. Talented veterans usually right the ship. It's called regression to the mean, and it's a tenet of statistics for a reason.

NO, REALLY, REMEMBER STATS 101. It's human to panic when a player expected to perform at a high level starts slow, especially when there's a rampaging free agent just waiting to help you replace him. Don't bail, at least not until a quarter to a third of the schedule has passed. It's called a valid sample size, and it's another tenet of statistics for a reason.

TAKE ANOTHER CHANCE. You don't want to give up on slumping giants too early, but you might want to grab a no-namer who's off to a fast start. Look at his owner's needs and offer a couple of relevant middle-of-your-roster names to make sure he bites.

NEVER GIVE UP. Early struggles are disheartening, but they're not fatal. Whatever the sport, there's almost always time to come back and finish strong.

FIGHT COMPLACENCY. You had the monster of all drafts and now your team has shot to the top of the standings. Nice job! But don't fall in love with your roster. Titles are secured with late-season moves. You can't simply sit back and wait for the trophy to come to you.

KNOW THERE'S ALWAYS NEXT YEAR. If you're in "keeper" or "dynasty" leagues—and thus can carry over some guys on your roster to next season—plan ahead. If you're at the bottom of the standings late in the year, offer players who'll help owners of still-competitive teams win now in exchange for their injured producers who will be valuable to you next season.

SPIN A BASKETBALL ON YOUR FINGER

Some people can walk on their hands. Others can recite full scenes from *DodgeBall* by heart. How will you wow the crowd? Here's one way.

1. Hold the ball, seams vertical, in front of you with your shooting hand in back and your nondominant hand in front, both elbows bent.

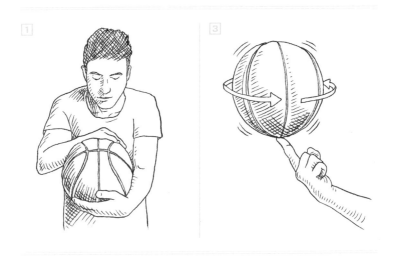

2. In one motion, spin the ball in the direction of your shooting hand as you gently toss it a few inches into the air. The spin is key: A fast but controlled effort keeps the ball close to your body and makes it easier to catch and balance.

3. As the ball begins to descend, position your dominant hand palm up, index finger extended. Reach slightly to meet the spinning ball—in the middle—on the pad of the outstretched digit. (Note: As you get better at this, you'll be able to toss the ball a little higher so you can catch it on the fingertip, but for now the pad will suffice.)

4. Keep the finger stiff and your bent elbow steady to offer a solid but flexible base on which the ball can continue its crowd-pleasing rotation.

CONGRATULATIONS!
YOU HAVE SUCCESSFULLY SPUN A BASKETBALL.

5. Once you've got it down, you'll want to try to keep the ball aloft by gently smacking it with your free hand in the direction it's spinning.

CONVERT A PENALTY KICK

ERIC WYNALDA
Former Forward, U.S. Men's National Soccer Team

Everybody says, "Don't look at the goalkeeper." I say something different. My theory is to think of the kick as a pass to a large target. You take a penalty kick from about 12 yards away. If you're making a 12-yard pass, you need to see where the defender is. You don't look at the ball; you look at the target. I trained myself to not look at the ball on penalty kicks. It's really hard, but a goalkeeper has a split second to read cues—the kicker's foot, his hips—before determining which way to go. If you get the keeper to hold his position just a bit longer, he won't have time to reach a ball hit with pace at a good spot. Or say you fake the keeper to dive one way so you can go the other. If your head is down, you can't see if the fake worked. Nowadays, most goalkeepers purposely stand off center, maybe a half step to the left, to get the kicker thinking he's giving up a whole side. They're counting on you to look down at the ball, so they can move back without you knowing. Basically, it leaves you to make a blind decision—Will he move or not?—and with uncertainty helps the goalkeeper. When your head is up, on the other hand, you keep control.

Again, I know every coach in America will tell you not to do what I am suggesting. They'll say you need to have a plan, pick your spot, focus on the ball, and make sure you execute. Hit it hard, hit it low. That part, at least, is right. The higher you aim, the greater the risk of hitting the ball over the goal. And goalkeepers have told me that it's harder for them to get down than to jump high. Still, I always got the feeling that making eye contact with them kind of freaked them out. *Why is this guy looking at me?* Plus, if they're looking at your eyes, they're not reading your hips and feet, right? I trust the keepers, and they say that waiting for me to kick drove them nuts.

STOP A PENALTY KICK

BRIANA SCURRY
Former Goalkeeper, U.S. Women's National Soccer Team

Players and coaches always argue with the referee after the call that sets up a penalty kick, so there are a couple of minutes to walk away from the goal to think about fundamentals and what you know about the kicker. I was always confident I could make the save if I read the kicker's cues. For example, if a predominantly right-footed kicker takes only a step or two away from the ball, at not too sharp an angle, it likely means she's going to hit it to the keeper's right. Of course, some players are cheeky about their run-up. They start and stop, they look at you or look down, waiting for you to move before deciding where to kick. In a lot of ways, the whole thing is a game of chicken, with kicker and keeper tracking each other. It's my advantage as soon as they show me where they're going. You'll see some keepers jumping side to side or waving their arms as the kicker sets up, hoping to influence the execution. I didn't do that. I thought of myself as a loaded spring, ready to pounce in either direction. If I'm jumping up and down, I'm not loaded.

Even with good preparation, though, saving a penalty kick is mostly guess-work. The great players know that if their kick is accurate, no keeper can stop it. But not all kickers are confident, so the mental game is critical. Psych out the kicker, and you have a chance. In a five-shot shoot-out, for example, if you get close to stopping a couple of early attempts, the remaining kickers will think they have to strike the ball even more precisely. The best part is, there's no pressure on the keeper because we're not expected to make the save. So block one in a shoot-out and you'll probably win. Block two and you're a legend!

AT THE POKER TABLE

Because if you can't spot "that guy" at the table, it's probably you.

DO	DON'T
Wait for your turn to bet or fold. Few things irk cardplayers more than someone playing out of turn.	Show your cards after a successful bluff. (Unless you're trying to get inside an opponent's head. Then it's fine. But don't gloat.)
Pile your wagered chips in front of you until all the betting for that round has been completed, then wait for the dealer to rake them—and everyone else's—into the middle.	Fling your chips toward the middle of the table, also known as "splashing the pot."
Know when it's your turn to deal, and get to it without being prompted.	Forget to shuffle the cards when you're done dealing, or forget to hand them to the second player to your left after the shuffle (assuming you're participating in a two-deck game).
Offer the person to your immediate left the opportunity to cut the shuffled deck before you deal.	Question another player's shuffling, unless it's clearly a part of the particular game's ethos. (Which, truth be told, it shouldn't be.)
Keep quiet after you've folded and further cards are revealed. Your reactions will either confuse or tip off other players.	Ask to "have a peek" at another's hidden cards once you've folded, unless you've witnessed regulars doing so first. And *never* look without asking.

DO	DON'T
Ask about "house rules" before you play the first hand at an unfamiliar game (e.g., do they frown on "sandbagging"—that is, checking then raising in the same round?).	Suggest adjustments or additions to house rules until you've played in a game at least a couple of times without incident.
Keep your feelings to yourself. Neither make light of nor be overly empathetic to another player's bad fortune. (An understated "bad beat" every once in a while is fine.)	Encourage strangers to play a hand that you're not participating in yourself. Come to think of it, don't do it even if you are.
Bring as much money as you're willing to lose and no more.	Ask to borrow money.

THROW OUT A FIRST PITCH

LEO MAZZONE
Former MLB Pitching Coach

Don't be a hero. You're throwing a ceremonial pitch, not trying to get the last out in the World Series. Don't throw from the pitcher's mound if you haven't practiced from there, or if you aren't sure you'll be able to reach home plate. There are Major League pitchers who have trouble hitting the catcher's mitt from that far, and you definitely don't want to bounce the damn thing!

Wherever you are throwing from, focus. Don't check out the fans in the stands; stare right at the chest of the guy you're throwing to. Grip the baseball on all four seams—that is, so the seams look like a sideways horseshoe—with the ball centered in your hand (see right). That will make it go straighter. And as you begin your motion, lift your leg and step right toward the catcher. Think of it as getting in position to throw a punch at your target.

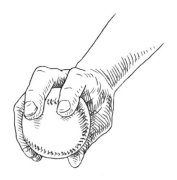

PROPOSE AT
A SPORTING EVENT

DON'T.*

---

*But if you must, don't use the scoreboard. A (slightly more) private proposal in the stands is (somewhat) more personal, generating in your section the attention and sense of community you seem to crave. (And there will still be plenty of people to take photos and/or make videos of your romantic gesture. There may even be a TV camera.) Above all, though, please (please) be as sure as you've ever been about anything in your life that your partner is going to say yes.

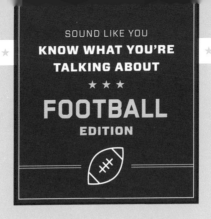

THREE TOPICS UP FOR DISCUSSION

1 HEAD TRAUMA

It turns out that repeatedly knocking your helmeted head at high speeds from childhood through young adulthood has serious long-term health consequences. It also turns out that the owners of football teams and presidents of colleges are just now beginning to take some responsibility for it.

2 COACHING DIVERSITY

The overwhelming majority of NFL players are black, the overwhelming majority of NFL head coaches are white. This might have something to do with the fact that pretty much all team owners are the latter (which is a whole other topic).

3 "STUDENT" ATHLETES

In aggregate, colleges generate billions of dollars in revenue from their football (and basketball) programs. Not enough of it goes to players, who are in theory rewarded with academic scholarships but whose degrees— in the rare cases that they're earned—are more often than not tainted by less-than-challenging coursework at best and grade inflation at worst. Maybe they should be paid as the "employees" they kind of are.

WHAT TO SAY WHEN . . .

. . . A RECEIVER DROPS A PASS:

"Next time they should try not to hit him in the hands!"

. . . AN UNDERDOG WINS:

"That's why they make them play the game."

. . . A TEAM APPEARS TO BE RUNNING UP THE SCORE:

"Guess [coach name]'s fantasy opponent this week started the [losing team]'s defense."

MARQUEE TEAMS: PROS AND CONS

NEW ENGLAND PATRIOTS

★ *Point of Pride:* The Patriot Way, a system-first ethos built atop an us-against-the-world, we-answer-to-no-one swagger fueled by a perfectionist coach.

✘ *Point of Contention:* A history of cheating scandals and rules bending that offends everyone but the faithful (and even some of them).

DALLAS COWBOYS

★ *Point of Pride:* An ongoing reign as "America's Team."

✘ *Point of Contention:* Until quite recently, their most consistent unit has been their cheerleaders.

PITTSBURGH STEELERS

★ *Point of Pride:* A blue-collar ethic and the most loyal fan base (Steeler Nation).

✘ *Point of Contention:* A reputation for dirty play, which is ironic given those annoying towels their fans love to wave.

Continued . . .

FOUR COACHES WHO MATTER

1 VINCE LOMBARDI

Because they named the Super Bowl trophy after the legendary Green Bay Packers coach (1959–1967).

2 BILL BELICHICK

Because no NFL coach has been to—or won—more Super Bowls.

3 PAUL "BEAR" BRYANT

Because it was said that the man who won six national college championships at Alabama could take his players and beat yours . . . or take yours and beat his. And that's saying something! Something no one has said—yet—about current Bama coach (and five-time national champ) Nick Saban.

4 JOE GIBBS

Because the Washington Redskins leader won each of the three Super Bowls he guided them to—with three different journeyman quarterbacks.

WHEN IN DOUBT, BRING UP . . .

JIM BROWN

The Cleveland Browns running back played in the 1950s and '60s, but he is still generally considered to be the best player ever, regardless of era.

SAMPLE CHATTER:
"If you ask me, no one can hold Jimmy Brown's cleats."

ONE DEBATE YOU CAN WIN

Should more teams go for it on fourth down?

THE PREMISE

It's been a fundamental tenet of the game for more than a century: gain 10 yards in four tries or relinquish the ball. But those four downs are generally whittled to three, with the fourth reserved for a punt that sends the ball to the opposing side on the offense's terms. The reasoning, long held and rarely explored, is this: Should the offense not achieve those 10 yards after that fourth play, the opposition starts its attack from a much more advantageous position than it would after a punt.

YOUR POSITION
Go for it!

YOUR ARGUMENT

Coaching staffs constantly rely on stats to inform their decisions, so why not this one? Numbers crunchers have definitively proven that in many cases the reward (a new first down) outweighs the risk (loss of ball). Indeed, in most every short-yardage scenario—3 yards or fewer—there need be no discussion, even if the alternative is almost-assured points from a routine field goal. Around midfield, forsaking a punt is worth considering with 5 or 6 yards to gain. Should the game situation—time left, score, etc.—be part of the calculus? Sure, although any also-ran team should go for it all the time, since they've really got nothing to lose. Will every failure bring on a bit of public shaming and media criticism for the coach? Sure, until a rebel confident enough to push back against "tradition" shows everyone else that they've been doing it wrong all along.

Continued . . .

A FEW FEARLESS FORECASTS TO MAKE

DEFINITELY!

The NFL, which already plays some regular-season games in London and Mexico City, will expand further into Europe and South America.

POSSIBLY . . .

Concern over concussions and related brain trauma will cause a growing number of parents to keep their children from playing football, shrinking the pool of competitive athletes and leaving the sport a shell of its former self.

WHY NOT?

After equipment improvements and changes in practice fail to make the sport safer, football will be banned in the United States and become an underground entertainment favored by gamblers and reprobates.

Fun Fact to Impress Your Friends

Q: Who's the only quarterback to start an NFL game without having started one in college?

A: Matt Cassel, for the Patriots, in 2008. After backing up Heisman Trophy winner Carson Palmer at USC, he subbed for an injured Tom Brady and led New England to an 11–4 record.

★ ★

GIVE A PEP TALK

BILL COLE
President, International Mental Game Coaching Association

Context matters. Are you playing a formidable opponent? Then you may need to give your team courage. If you're playing a weaker one, getting your guys to focus might be more important. You also have to determine what's needed. Each sport and each game is different, but most athletes need revving down, not revving up. They're already too wired.

Motivating teams, however, is difficult. Half may love what you say and the other half may not. So be honest. Tell them, "I'm going to give you ten things to think about. Take what you need, and let go of the rest." Most coaches don't do that. I also start with an "attitude of gratitude," reminding them how fortunate they are to be able to compete in a sport they love. It goes a long way toward reducing the stress of a big event and helps to emphasize opportunity rather than expectation. We constantly throw expectations at athletes: "You're gonna win!" and "You're gonna be number 1!" I prefer an approach that's process focused, not outcome focused: "Just play your game and see what happens" or "Put yourself in a situation where you can do something memorable."

You should also remind them of the work they've done. "Trust your training" is a phrase I use a lot. I also say, "Don't force it. Let your preparation take over." Hearing that is a relief to athletes. You're not going to change technique or improve skill level in those last pregame moments. Instead, emphasize strengths; that's what builds confidence. You want the opponent worrying about your team, not your team worrying about the opponent.

Finally, don't underestimate the benefits of props. A well-chosen song or film clip can help you create the mind-set you want to instill.

KEEP SCORE IN BOWLING

A large percentage of humankind doesn't know how to fill in a bowling score sheet, enough so that there are few establishments left that don't feature automatic scoring machines at each alley. But that's no excuse. It works like this:

Each "frame" consists of as many as two rolls, the goal of each being to knock down as many pins as possible. But if it were simply a matter of knocking down all ten pins in each frame of a ten-frame game, a perfect score would be 100. Of course, it's not. Rather, it's 300, and the key to understanding this strange fact is understanding how strikes (all ten pins knocked down by the first roll) and spares (all ten pins knocked down after the second roll) work. The scores for both accomplishments are in fact determined by the results of the *subsequent* roll or, in the case of strikes, rolls. When you roll a strike, your score for that frame is 10 plus the score in the subsequent two frames; when you roll a spare, your score for the frame is 10 plus the score in one subsequent frame. Here's how it plays out.

ELLAND ROAD LANES

NAME	1	2	3	10	FINAL SCORE
Posh	X · 7 / · 9 −				
	20 · 39 · 48				
Becks	3 4 · 2 / · 6 −				
	7 · 17 · 23				

In the chart opposite, the first bowler rolled a strike in frame 1, marked by an "X" in the corner box. The main box is left blank until succeeding frames are bowled. Had she thrown a pair of gutter balls in frame 2, the scorer would have written "10" in the main box of frame 1 (10 pins + 0 + 0) and the same in frame 2, as no more pins were knocked down. But because our strike-thrower rolled a spare in frame 2—denoted by a diagonal line in that corner box—the scorer added 10 from that frame to the 10 already earned, and marked a 20 in frame 1. Moving forward, the score recorded for our bowler in frame 2 was likewise determined by the first ball she rolled in frame 3, a 9. So her score in frame 2 was 39: 20 (from frame 1) + 10 (from her spare in frame 2) + 9 (from her first roll in frame 3) = 39.

A perfect score of 300 is achieved by rolling only strikes. So had our bowler rolled a strike in frame 2, the scorer would have left both frames 1 and 2 unmarked until the results of the third frame were registered. Had she rolled a strike in frame 3, the scorer would have marked a 30 in frame 1, waiting until the results of frame 4 to apply the retroactive math to frame 2. And so on. Ten strikes in a row—plus two more strikes in the rolls earned to fill out the final frame—gets her to 300.

STAY ON A BUCKING BRONCO

CLINT WELLS
Bareback Director, Pacific Northwest Professional Rodeo Association

Winning a rodeo competition is about more than just staying on a horse for eight seconds. It's about form. When they open the gate, you want to have your spurs up over the horse's shoulders. So when the gate opens, you're essentially straddling his neck with your legs straight (a) until he takes his first jump, or "marks out," and that's when you roll your spurs back to your rigging—that strap around the torso (b). Then, as he comes down, you roll them up over his shoulders again. You repeat this over and over, in a rhythm, while keeping your upper body straight. That's important because the judge will be looking at all of it: how well you spur the horse, how hard the horse bucks, and how much control you have in keeping your body square.

The best riders I've ever seen have something I call "controlled aggression." If you're tense or distracted, the horse will have the advantage. To really ride a rank horse, you have to find that burning fire in you and take the fight to him—or the horse will rip you right out of your rigging. Steven Peebles, the 2016 world champion, is so aggressive you can actually see his feet pause for a moment on the horse's neck while he's spurring. That means he's ahead of the horse, in control of the rhythm of the ride.

TEAM NAMES

THE QUESTION

Six team names are repeated among the four major North American sports leagues. What are they?

THE ANSWER

1. Cardinals
   (Arizona, NFL; St. Louis, MLB)

2. Giants
   (New York, NFL; San Francisco, MLB)

3. Jets
   (New York, NFL; Winnipeg, NHL)

4. Kings
   (Los Angeles, NHL; Sacramento, NBA)

5. Panthers
   (Carolina, NFL; Florida, NHL)

6. Rangers
   (New York, NHL; Texas, MLB)

WIN AT
ROCK-PAPER-SCISSORS

Because there is actually a way to skew the odds of everyone's favorite "random" decision-making game in your favor.

PEDDLE INFLUENCE. When challenging an opponent—particularly a beginner—subtly flash "scissors" when recounting the rules. Your suggestion will become their action, which is why you will bust out the rock and crush 'em!

LOOK FOR TELLS. Amateurs tend to simultaneously rotate their elbow out and turn their forearm in when planning to throw paper. Which is when you will throw scissors and cut 'em!

FIGHT POWER WITH POWER. Newbies rarely throw paper on their first go, equating it with weakness. So the safest first throw against them is rock. In the best-case scenario, it wins (against scissors), and at worst, it ties (with another rock).

PLAY MIND GAMES. Telling your opponent you're expecting her to throw rock is a good way of making sure she either doesn't (if she hates being predictable) or does (if she hates being manipulated). Rely on this tactic if you know your foe well.

PLAN AHEAD. During multiple-throw contests (e.g., best two out of three), you can keep an opponent from getting inside *your* head by settling on a throwing sequence beforehand.

GO BEHIND YOUR BACK. There's nothing in the rules that says you have to keep your competing hand in front of you before the "rock, paper, scissors, throw!" count. So don't.

SNEAK DOWN TO BETTER SEATS

It costs plenty just to get through the gates of most major sporting events. But *really* good seats? You'll be sitting in those only if you're willing to eat cereal for dinner for a month. Unless, that is, you snag a couple of relatively affordable nosebleed seats, then finagle your way into the prime real estate. Officially, teams frown on it. Unofficially, they often let it happen if you're discreet—and the actual ticket owners aren't around. So though you didn't hear it from us, here's how to do it right.

DO ADVANCE SCOUTING. Before you head to the park, scan secondary-market ticket websites to see which sections have the most seats for sale. Some of those are likely to go unsold—and thus will be vacant.

BRING YOUR TOOLS. Binoculars or a camera with a zoom lens will help you spy on potentially available targets once you're inside.

SETTLE FOR PARTIAL VICTORIES. At basketball or hockey games, upgrade only during halftime or between periods. Ushers in many arenas don't check ticket stubs once the game is under way, so you will likely be able to join the crowd as everyone files back to their seats after hitting the head or the concession stand.

ROOT FOR THE HOME TEAM. Don't wear enemy colors. It draws unnecessary attention.

ACT LIKE YOU BELONG. Some people really can afford those exorbitant front-row seats, and they can sniff out those who don't seem like they can too. So don't boast about paying cheap-seat prices once you're in the fancy section.

KEEP YOUR HANDS FULL. When you make your move, head down the aisle with a couple of beers or a box of snacks. Ushers are less likely to ask to see the ticket of someone thus occupied.

PRAY FOR A BLOWOUT. When a game's result is no longer in doubt, many fans leave to beat the rush. Ask someone abandoning a desirable section for his stub. There is no better way in; you can't be turned away if you hold proof of seat ownership.

TAKE NOTES. Think of every upgrade as a recon mission. Do you like the sight lines, or would you rather be a couple of sections to the left? Are you sitting next to season ticket holders who don't make it to every game? (There's no harm in chatting up your neighbors.) What doesn't get you kicked out makes you smarter next time around.

WHEN ALL ELSE FAILS . . . Far be it from us to encourage bribery, but we'd be derelict if we didn't mention that the wrong ticket stub with the right $20 bill often does the trick, particularly when it's gilded with a sob story: "I'm trying to impress my date—can you help me out?" or "It's my kid's first game." Ushers are human. Most of them, anyway.

THROW A WIFFLE CURVE

It's a backyard game, but it still needs a resident ace. There will be nobody staring you down as the ball clears the fence if you perfect this unhittable pitch.

1. Buy a Wiffle ball—a real one, with the trademark—and a thin yellow bat.

2. Read the instructions on the side of the box.

3. Come to grips with the fact that steps 1 and 2 are the easy part. Throwing accurate curves requires patience and perseverance.

4. Grip the ball—index and middle finger on top (see right)—with the holes facing "inside" (closer to your ear) for a curve that should break down and away from a right-handed batter. Hold it facing "outside" for a slider that should break down and in. (The opposite is true for lefties, both on the mound and in the batter's box.)

5. Wind up and pitch, remembering that it's all in the wrist. That is, a quick downward snap as you release is what gives breaking balls "bite," thus avoiding—or at least reducing—the possibility that the ball will "hang" in the strike zone. (Note: Don't throw as hard as you can; it could hurt your shoulder or elbow and, anyway, tends to reduce the wrist snap.)

6. Repeat step 5 endlessly. But until you get out there and try it—against the garage door, a fence, or, ideally, a plastic lawn chair (aim for the backrest)—you won't know what works best for you. It's worth figuring out, though, if only so you can be the Cy Young of picnics forevermore.

A BASEBALL GAME AT THE BALLPARK

Conventional Wisdom: There's no better place to settle in with a beer and a hot dog than ground level behind home plate; from there, you can both scan the full field and zero in on pitch movement.

For Your Consideration: Position yourself down either baseline, at ground level and toward the outfield; you can still see all of the action, but there's a much better chance of finding yourself in position to catch a foul ball (see page 17).

SNAG AN AUTOGRAPH

Autograph hunting is no halfhearted endeavor. For starters, athletes are a constantly harassed and thus short-tempered lot. Plus, at any given moment you are almost assuredly not the only one making the ask, so maximizing your chances of success requires a bit of a script.

DON'T LEAVE IT TO FATE. The best tactic is to be where athletes are accessible. Follow the men and women who interest you on social media. If they've been scheduled for a signing nearby, you'll find out there first. Unfortunately, such opportunities are rare.

BE WELL STOCKED . . . You don't want to be stuck with a dirty napkin or your sister's neon green softball the day your favorite athlete decides to visit with fans. Always carry a suitably signable object with you. Whatever it is should be in good condition. Athletes are meticulous; presentation matters to them.

. . . AND WELL ARMED. Test your pen (Sharpies work best) at home; heaven forbid you're inkless when opportunity knocks. For potential multiple-athlete situations like spring training or pro-am golf tournaments, bring extra implements. You don't want to miss one guy because another happens to be using your only pen.

GET AHEAD OF THE GAME. If you're heading to the stadium, arrive early. The window of possibility is small, almost exclusively limited to pre-game workouts. Be early to off-field appearances too; nothing is worse than spending hours on a line worrying about whether you're going to get what you came for.

KNOW THE SITUATION. Is it a particularly important game? Then you shouldn't be bothering the players. Even on regular game days, it's a waste of time to stalk the starting pitcher or goalie before he hits the field.

FOLLOW THE (RIGHT) CROWD. You know who gets what they want? Cute kids and attractive women. Find a group heavy with either and do your best to blend in.

BE LOUD—BUT DON'T FORGET YOUR MANNERS. When you get close, make it clear what you're after. But don't be demanding, especially if the athlete waves you off. Two things to remember: (1) You're asking for a favor, so be respectful; and (2) insulted athletes never forget.

SHOW YOU CARE. With only a few seconds to make your case, you need to prove that you're a real fan and not just looking for a potential investment. If you're young enough, wear a jersey (if you're chasing someone in particular, wear his), and when the player looks your way, be ready with something personal to say—a compliment for his recent exploits, maybe, or a comment about his favorite band.

MAKE FRIENDS. Most serious collectors can't wait to brag about their conquests, and what they say can help you down the line. Chances are, the fellow autograph seeker who looks the most prepared is the guy with the intel. (Where do visiting teams stay when they're in town? Where is that injured player sitting in the stands?) Tell him what you know, and he'll likely tell you what he knows.

MAKE A QUICK GETAWAY. Got yours? Good. Now leave so others can get theirs. Besides, you don't want to linger long enough for your hard-won item to get crushed by the crowd.

STOP A PENALTY SHOT

MARTIN BRODEUR
Retired NHL Goaltender

What hand is he shooting with? Because that dictates your positioning. Also watch his head. Some guys look at you and some don't, but their eyes will show if they're going to shoot or deke. If a guy is staring at you, he's looking for a hole, a place to shoot the puck. If he's not, he's going to throw a fake or try to surprise you with a quick shot. Of course, you have to focus on the puck eventually. If it's in front of him, most times that means he's going to deke. If it's on the side, usually he's going to shoot. And you have to pay attention to how fast the shooter is skating. You should be setting up high in the goal crease, but you don't want him to get around you, so you have to gauge his speed to keep the same distance between you and the puck at all times.

Finally, it's always good to try to play mind games. If I could grab the shooter's attention—if he looked at me—I might wave my glove or change my stance. Maybe I'd stand up straight and lean on my stick like, *I'm just resting*. You do this to break the other guy's focus, to get him to think, *What is he doing?* But then you get right back in position. Mostly I also tried to look like I was giving him something he thought he could take advantage of. Like, I lowered my glove so the shooter would think, *He's giving me the top corner*, and try to beat me there. That would often backfire on him.

WHEN YOU HECKLE

Because everyone in the stands thinks "that guy" is a jackass.

DO	DON'T
Get athletes thinking. A distracted rival is an advantage for your team.	Get athletes angry. A motivated rival is a disadvantage for your team.
Go after college and pro athletes.	Go after high school athletes, unless you're a high schooler yourself. (Lay off even younger athletes entirely, however old you are.)
Research your target. Nothing hits home harder than a reference to, say, a particularly humiliating loss.	Reference players' personal tragedy and the like. Because then you're not a heckler, you're just a bad person.
Wait for quiet moments. What good is heckling if it can't be heard?	Consider the concerned silence caused by an injured player "a quiet moment."
Be clever (e.g., with smart wordplay).	Be vulgar.
Focus on rookies and substitutes. The less battle-tested are usually the most vulnerable.	Waste your time on superstars. They long ago learned to tune out the noise.
Rely on props. A dry-erase board that allows for reactive smack will be appreciated by fans and athletes alike.	Rely on the beer man. Incomprehensibility is counterproductive.

BE A GOOD SPORTS PARENT

STEVE WULF
Editor, Fathers & Sons & Sports

The aspiration here is intentionally moderate. Forget about "great" or "ideal." The aim is to be "good," which really means not being "bad." Everybody makes mistakes. I say this as an imperfect father of four kids who played ten sports and gave our family memories to make us smile for the rest of our lives. Here's what I've learned.

IT'S NOT ABOUT YOU. It's about her, or him, or them. Take pride in what your child does, but be mindful of his or her needs, wishes, and hopes. So what if she's not Alex Morgan, or he's not Mike Trout, or they're not the Golden State Warriors? Children are not out there for your reflected glory. They're out there to learn how to play a sport, wear a uniform, make new friends, and discover the joys of being part of a team.

STOP TYING THEIR SHOES. This is not a metaphor. I've seen a lot of parents bending over to lace up the cleats, skates, etc., of their little jocks. Much better to teach them how, empowering them to do it themselves. One of the most awesome sights is watching an eight-year-old hockey player tie her own skates and tape her own stick. Not to mention, the coach wants you out of the way so he or she can talk to the players. The earlier you take this advice, the better.

TAKE JOYRIDES. Make the trip to and from the game a happy time. That means letting the kids control the conversation and the music. Post-victory rides usually take care of themselves. But if, after a loss, the kids complain about a coach or a teammate, explain (gently) that griping about someone else does not help the team, and all they can control is their own effort. Then point out what they did in the game that you liked.

BRING PLENTY OF BUTTER. This *is* a metaphor. If you must note a mistake, make sure your critique is sandwiched by specific praise. That's a 2-to-1 ratio of praise to criticism. Never let the negatives outnumber the positives.

MIND THE VOCALS . . . You're in the stands to cheer. That's all. So think before you yell, "You're blind, Blue!" or "Call it both ways!" at an official, and never—ever—direct frustration at a player or a coach. They can't hear you, anyway, but their relatives sitting next to you can.

. . . BUT KNOW WHEN (AND HOW) TO SPEAK UP. Most coaches are as dedicated to the welfare of their players as they are to their win-loss record. But sometimes you will encounter a situation in which your child is not being treated fairly. You could fume in silence or pull your child off the team, but there's a third option: Approach the coach and calmly ask why your kid is riding the bench or not getting an opportunity to pitch. Chances are, the coach will respond in kind, and together you can figure out a way to improve your kid's skills, effort, or understanding of the game. And if the coach says something along the lines of "I'm the coach; I make the decisions," then talk—again, rationally—to a league authority to whom he or she does have to answer. There are life lessons for your kids in how *you* deal with conflict and unfairness.

IGNORE THE TROPHY BACKLASH. You hear this a lot nowadays, usually from a former pro who's now on TV in a suit: "I don't want my kid getting a trophy just for participating." As if a little plastic token will make a kid soft. Look, it's a memento of a time worth cherishing. Participation trophies aren't for the stars—believe me, the kids know who's good—they're for the players who shine by showing up. And that's worth something. As a former coach, my favorite time of the season was when I gave out trophies and said a few words about each of the recipients. It should be your favorite time too.

BREAK IN A GLOVE

Not all baseball or softball gloves come off the shelf game-ready. Many need to be softened and sculpted to fit the owner's hands and fielding needs. It's not a particularly subtle process, and yet there is something of an art to it, not to mention a line to navigate between supple and saggy. Here are five methods that have earned the serious ballplayers' seal of approval.

> *Note: When the directives below call for the use of a ball, make sure to use a sport-appropriate choice. That is, if you're breaking in a softball glove, use a softball; for a baseball glove, use a Major League hardball.*

1. **SLEEP ON IT.** Sticking a glove under your mattress—with a ball tucked inside the webbing—helps establish a deep pocket while you get your beauty rest. Be sure to check the glove each morning, adjusting the fold as needed to prevent creasing. Three to five nights should do it.

2. **TRUSS IT.** With a ball in the webbing, roll the "pinky" so it tucks inside the top corner of the pocket. Then wrap tightly with rubber bands or shoelaces. Again, three to five nights should be enough. (Note: Combine this with the mattress trick above for maximum results.) That said, ballplayers have recently begun to flare the thumb outward instead of rolling it inward, to offer a wider opening to receive the ball. Want to try it? Just bend the reinforced thumb back a bit.

3. **LATHER IT.** There is no shortage of specialty oils out there—many gloves come with recommendations for specific types. Too much of it, though, can stain your glove and actually soften it too much, making it less likely to stand firm against hard-hit balls. An alternative: Before

trussing your glove (see above), massage a dollop of shaving cream—the foamy, white, unscented kind—into the pocket.

4. **STEAM IT.** This is a common trick in many Major League clubhouses. Steaming a glove over boiling water (you can use a vegetable steamer) opens the pores of the leather, making it softer and easier to work into shape. Similarly, you can soak the glove in warm water for a minute or so, then throw it into a clothes dryer for about ten minutes.

5. **PLAY WITH IT.** Of course, the simplest way to break in a glove is to catch with it—again and again. No, it's not the most efficient way, and, yes, your fingers will ache from squeezing the rigid rawhide. But each time the ball hits the pocket, the glove will mold a bit more to your hand and catching style.

THROW A SPIRAL

AARON RODGERS
NFL Quarterback

Everybody has a different way of gripping the ball, and it changes as you age and your hands get bigger. When I was young, I put two full fingers on the laces. Now I have just one: my pinky, between the third and fourth lace from the top—the back of the ball. My ring finger touches a lace but doesn't sit on it. More important, though, than how many fingers are on the laces—some quarterbacks use two or even three—is making sure the palm is not flat against the football. You throw the ball with grip strength from your fingers—the thumb and middle finger, specifically—so it's important

to maintain space between palm and ball. The index finger should be last to touch the ball; it's the guiding/snapping finger.

Ultimately, that snap is everything. For a right-handed quarterback, it means snapping down and to the left as you throw (see below); vice versa for a left-hander. When I was in middle school, I heard a trick that has stuck with me: Pretend you're a cowboy replacing your six-shooter in a holster on your opposing hip. So if you're a right-hander, you snap your wrist down and to the left as you release. Your thumb will be heading for your left hip as you follow through.

One more thing: People think you have to throw with high velocity, but a perfect spiral is really about the spin. A ball that is spiraling fast without a lot of velocity is very catchable. A ball that isn't spinning will wobble, making it harder to catch. Which brings us back to the wrist flick. A good flick creates a great spiral.

FILL OUT AN NCAA TOURNAMENT BRACKET

College basketball's postseason tournament traffics in a unique blend of on-court uncertainty and off-court interest. But that combination means the odds of finishing atop the leaderboard of any March Madness pool can be intimidatingly long—whether you know what offensive efficiency is or you can't tell the Bulldogs from the Huskies. These let-history-be-your-guidelines will help you keep your dreams alive.

DO AN HOUR'S WORTH OF HOMEWORK. Even if you know nothing about college basketball beyond the fact that everybody hates Duke, you can still fill out a respectable pool bracket with barely any effort. Start with a Google search for "NCAA Tourney predictions" to see what the experts are thinking. Who is vulnerable to an early defeat? Who is riding a hot streak? Whatever your resident office hoops head might imply, after doing a little cramming you will basically have as much chance to win as somebody who's been following the sport for decades.

NEVER PICK A NUMBER 16 SEED TO BEAT A NUMBER 1. Yes, the impossible may happen someday, but as of this writing, it hasn't yet. If you're feeling reckless, pick a number 2 to beat a 1 in the first round. It's rare but not preposterous.

ALWAYS CHOOSE ONE 12–5 UPSET. In these matchups, the lower-seeded team wins often enough to justify the gamble.

CHOOSE A FEW OTHER UPSETS . . . Of your initial thirty-two first-round picks, it's fine—even wise—to pick six to eight lower seeds to defeat their higher-regarded competition. But don't be any more unconventional than that. (Here's a bit more wiggle room for the favorite-phobic among you: Don't count as upsets the 9-seeds you've chosen over 8s; those games are toss-ups.)

. . . BUT DON'T EXPECT THEM TO GO FAR. Casual fans especially fall in love with the idea of a Cinderella winning it all, or at least cracking the Sweet Sixteen, Elite Eight, or Final Four. That's partly because historically when such teams do well, they get tons of media attention, and that makes their success seem more common than it is. But they get all that media attention precisely because such occurrences are so unusual. From 2005 through 2016, you know how many teams seeded lower than 3 won it all? One. So penciling in two double-digit seeds in the Sweet Sixteen, and maybe no further, seems more than sufficient.

FOLLOW THE TALENT. Most title teams feature at least two players who are projected to go in the first round of the next NBA draft. Google "NBA Mock Draft" and cross-reference the listed names with tournament rosters.

DON'T OVERDOSE ON 1-SEEDS. Conservative bracketologists may be tempted to pick nothing but 1 to advance to the Final Four. But that has happened once since 1985. That said, be sure you have at least one number 1 among the four last-standing teams. Since 1985, they've been shut out of the final weekend just twice.

> *Note: Think about entering more than one bracket, but only if each one is different enough to justify the additional expense. To be clear, you're doing this not so much because you'll be any more likely to win the pool, but because it will increase your odds of remaining in the running a bit longer, which will keep you engaged and give you something to talk about with everyone else who's suddenly a college basketball fan.*

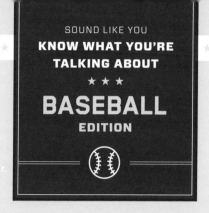

THREE TOPICS UP FOR DISCUSSION

1 PERFORMANCE-ENHANCING DRUGS

Nearly two decades after the game's steroid use became national news, players continue to test positive for banned substances of all kinds. Although fewer stars have been implicated of late, breakout seasons still provoke skepticism, a side effect of the original scandal that may never fade.

2 PAY TO STAY

As in all major U.S. sports, baseball owners are very good at getting locals to pay for new stadiums, often by threatening to move if they don't. This benefits owners, but few of their fellow citizens.

3 WHERE ARE THE BLACK BASEBALL PLAYERS?

There's been a dramatic fall in the number of African Americans in Major League Baseball, despite efforts by the sport to create grassroots interest.

WHAT TO SAY WHEN . . .

. . . A MANAGER GETS EJECTED FROM A GAME:

"They should eject all of them until they start wearing street clothes like coaches do in every other sport."

. . . AN ANNOUNCER EXPLAINS THAT A PITCHER INTENTIONALLY HIT A BATTER TO "SEND A MESSAGE":

"And that message is, 'Baseball players have the maturity of fourth graders.'"

. . . A PITCHER IS CALLED FOR A BALK:

"Ten dollars to the first person who can explain the balk rule without Googling it."

MARQUEE TEAMS: PROS AND CONS

NEW YORK YANKEES

⭐ *Point of Pride:* The most league pennants and world championships in MLB history.

✖ *Point of Contention:* A singular sense of entitlement that manifests as an annoying expectation that a World Series win isn't so much earned as owed.

ST. LOUIS CARDINALS

⭐ *Point of Pride:* The "Cardinal Way," an approach that stresses fundamentals and selflessness, resulting in the most world championships of any National League team.

✖ *Point of Contention:* A fan base that dismisses American League baseball—forty-plus years after its adoption of the designated hitter rule.

BOSTON RED SOX

⭐ *Point of Pride:* The perseverance to endure a century-long "curse" to win three World Series titles in the first years of the twenty-first century.

✖ *Point of Contention:* Let's just say recent success has gone to their heads.

Continued . . .

THREE BALLPARKS THAT MATTER

1 FENWAY PARK

The home of the Red Sox is the oldest ballpark in the major leagues, having been opened in 1912. But it is known as much as anything for having the tallest outfield wall: the "Green Monster" in left field. FYI: It was blue until 1947.

2 WRIGLEY FIELD

The home of the Chicago Cubs is the oldest ballpark in the National League—debuting just a bit later than Fenway, in 1914—and the last to have installed lights for night games (in 1988). No other active MLB stadium has hosted more NFL games, by the way. (The Bears played there from 1921 to 1970.)

3 CAMDEN YARDS

For decades, new MLB stadiums had a soulless sameness. That trend was reversed when this retro-style park debuted in Baltimore in 1992, evoking a pre–World War II era when ballyards were smaller and better fit the contours of urban neighborhoods. Almost every stadium built since is a descendant of what is officially known as Oriole Park at Camden Yards.

WHEN IN DOUBT, BRING UP . . .

HANK AARON

Although Babe Ruth is arguably the best and surely the most famous baseball player ever, the Braves' slugging outfielder, unlike the Babe, set his records when the sport was integrated.

SAMPLE CHATTER:
"The best ever? You mean aside from Hank Aaron?"

Is the designated hitter rule good for baseball?

THE PREMISE

In 1973, the American League adopted a rule that allows one player to bat in place of the pitcher throughout the game. The so-called designated hitter (DH) rule has divided fans ever since. Those who favor the DH believe it makes the game more exciting by replacing ineffectual hitters (i.e., most pitchers) with accomplished batsmen.

YOUR POSITION
Nope.

YOUR ARGUMENT

Baseball makes claims of being America's national pastime, and nothing is more American than a meritocracy. While pinch-hitting is a core part of the game, players should otherwise earn the right to bat by playing in the field. Moreover, if increased offense is the goal of the DH rule, one can logically argue that all batters and fielders should be specialists, focusing only on their primary skill, much as football morphed from so-called two-way players, who served on both offense and defense, to those specializing in one or the other.

A FEW FEARLESS FORECASTS TO MAKE

DEFINITELY!
The Cubs will become a dynasty. (Seriously, it just has to happen.)

Continued . . .

POSSIBLY . . .

Concerned by waning interest and the outsized importance of relief pitchers, MLB will radically adjust its rules—say, contracting from nine to seven innings— to create a shorter version of the game.

WHY NOT?

MLB will legalize every conceivable performance-enhancing drug. After a few years of renewed interest in comically absurd final scores and performances, fans will disappear for good.

Fun Fact to Impress Your Friends

In the early days of baseball, gamblers often bet in groups, known as pools. Many of these gamblers attended early professional games, sitting together in what was called the "pool-box." In an attempt to clean up the game, league officials banished these scallywags, forcing them to congregate in saloons and billiards parlors, which soon enough began to be called "pool parlors." That's why most Americans now call the common fifteen-ball game of billiards "pool."

★ ★

WIN BEST IN SHOW

BONNIE THRELFALL
English Cocker Spaniel Breeder and Handler

Here's the thing about showing dogs: Proper show behavior can be taught in a month by an experienced handler, but it won't mean anything if you don't start with an outstanding specimen. Like all dog lovers, people new to owning and showing tend to be ruled by their hearts. They fall in love with that boxer and buy him because in their mind he is a model of the breed. But succeeding at shows means understanding the defined standards completely, and that takes at least a year of dispassionate study, going to as many shows as possible that feature your breed. (Don't take your own dog.) Talk to owners and handlers to really learn the criteria.

As far as handling your dog in the ring, don't overtrain him in the month before the show. It's a classic novice move that speaks to the anxiety of the handler. And, really, that is what makes the difference: Any competition, especially Best in Show, is won or lost on *human* behavior, not canine behavior. Dogs sense it when you tighten up. Most of them would have the time of their lives during shows—who wouldn't love all that play and attention?—as long as a nervous handler on the other end of the leash didn't distract them. Worse, such an experience will create a negative association with the ring for the future. When you're in the ring, stay relaxed.

BLUFF

DANIEL NEGREANU
Multiple World Series of Poker Bracelet Winner

Before you think about bluffing at the poker table, you need to ask yourself two questions. The first is: *Whom am I trying to bluff?* That matters, because if you are up against a player who barely understands the game or the strength of his own hand, there's a possibility he won't even be aware that he should fold to your bluff. Bluffing is about telling a story—about convincing someone through betting that you have certain cards—but if your opponent doesn't understand the language you're speaking, he will be oblivious to your story. The second question requires self-awareness: *How does my opponent perceive me?* In other words, will this person trust the story you want to tell? Does she think that you bet only when you have a good hand? Has she seen you bluff a lot already? If your opponent sees you as angry because you've been losing or reckless because you don't care, she isn't going to buy your bluff. On the other hand, if she thinks you're a straight shooter who always tells a believable story with your betting, you just might get away with your fiction. So you need to know how you present at the table. The key to bluffing is to know your opponent *and* yourself.

TAKE A DIVE

DON'T.*

---

*It is a scourge in soccer, a growing nuisance in the NBA, and downright lame in the NHL. When a catcher frames a pitch so the ump calls a ball a strike, that's tactical (see page 138). But when, after barely being brushed by a defender, a halfback tumbles to the ground to steal a free kick? That's just tacky.

THROW A DART

Darts is an ancient game, played first by soldiers killing time between killing times. (They tossed blades at overturned tree trunks, hence the rings of modern dart boards.) Sometime around World War I, the game moved indoors to pubs throughout England, where locals tossed their projectiles at keg lids affixed to the wall (hence the bull's-eye—aka "cork"—in the center).

Though many variations of the game have emerged since, two constants hold for them all: (1) The bull's-eye must be 5 feet 8 inches off the floor; and (2) the throw, or "toe," line must be 7 feet 9.25 inches from the board.

Darts rewards accuracy. Here's how to stay on target.

STAND STRONG. Sure footing is essential, but one stance does not fit all. Most folks prefer to stand either "face-front" (shoulders parallel to board) or "sideways" (shoulders perpendicular). Whichever method feels right to you, your feet should be far enough apart to provide a solid base. And once you find a comfortable stance, stick with it, to build muscle memory.

EYE THE PRIZE. Just as most of us are either left-handed or right-handed, we also have a dominant eye. To determine which is yours, alternate closing one of them when you throw. Whichever is harder to keep shut is the dominant one. That's the eye you should use to aim.

HOLD ON LOOSELY. There is no proper way to grip a dart. (Often, though, a three-finger hold—thumb, index, middle—feels right.) There is a proper grip *pressure*, however: the more relaxed, the better. Darts is a game of touch, not force.

DRAW THE LINE OF FIRE. Point your lead foot directly at the target. Even if you stand face-front, one foot should be slightly ahead. In either case, the lead foot is generally the right one for righties and the left for lefties. Place a bit more weight on that leg as you raise your throwing arm so the dart and dominant eye align with the target.

LET FLY! Again, easy does it. Consider: Even a small child has the strength to make this throw. Maintain arm movement in a two-dimensional plane; that is, simply forward and back. Cutting down on extraneous sideways movement lessens the room for error. Angle the dart tip slightly up throughout the throw. Most throws made by inexperienced players land far below the intended target.

JUGGLE A PUCK

Maybe you're not the smoothest of backward skaters. And maybe your slap shot scares no one. But you can still impress on the ice with this bit of stick-and-puck dexterity.

1. Find yourself a hockey puck and stick. Any hard surface will do as a practice venue, although, of course, the ice is the most appropriate.

2. Holding the stick normally and with the puck in front of you, lean down and press the front side of the stick blade almost flat on the puck. Use the heel or toe of the blade, but avoid the middle.

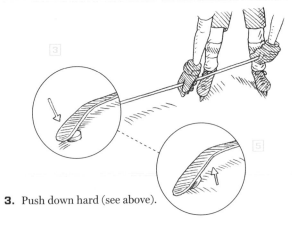

3. Push down hard (see above).

4. Harder!

5. If you've pushed hard enough, the puck will begin to lift off the surface, as if drawn by a magnet to your stick blade (see above).

6. As the puck begins to lift, scoop it in a single, fluid motion, by flipping the blade over so that it's under the puck (see 6a below) , lifting it, as if you were presenting a gift to, say, a king or perhaps Lord Stanley (see 6b below).

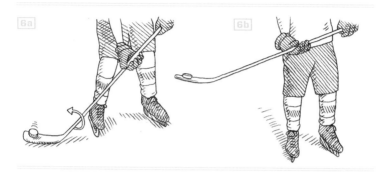

7. Once the puck is on your blade, pop it in the air by pushing your forward hand up in a short but firm gesture. If you do this correctly—which you will, eventually—the puck will lift a few inches. That's what you want, because then you can . . .

8. Catch it! And by that we mean bring your stick blade to where it was before you popped it up and wait there for the puck. Keep your arm a bit loose so when the puck drops on the blade, it is met with the slightest "give."

9. Try it a few more times. Scoop, pop, catch. Once that's perfected, try to replace "catch" with "pop," as in scoop-pop-pop. Keep at it until you get it down.

CONGRATULATIONS!
YOU HAVE SUCCESSFULLY JUGGLED A HOCKEY PUCK.

10. Continue adding "pops" until you're ready to impress your fellow rinkrats.

RUN A PICKUP GAME

DARREN CHERVITZ
Commissioner, Fourth Down League

Every Sunday morning from Labor Day through March, a dozen or so guys across a wide range of ages, ethnicities, races, nationalities, religions, sexual orientations, and socioeconomic backgrounds gather on a well-worn field on the west side of Manhattan to participate in an epic battle of touch football. It hasn't been easy keeping the game going over the years, but the seventy-five or so people who have cycled through the FDL are united by a motto, "Recreational goodness by any means necessary," and a keen awareness of the fact that a regular game on a crowded island is a rare privilege. At least that's what I tell myself as I consider how my commishly duties have safeguarded our decade-plus longevity. To safeguard yours, do what I do:

DICTATE BENEVOLENTLY. Early on, I ran the FDL as a democracy—USA! USA!—and it was a huge mistake. Our game nearly imploded several times over issues grown men with full lives shouldn't care about. I now find myself assuming the stance of a fair but authoritarian ruler. It's not that I don't listen to players' input; it's that I've come to realize that mostly they just want to know that someone moderately competent is in charge.

PUNISH CONSISTENTLY. Even the most harmonious group of athletic comrades contains otherwise well-meaning individuals who arrive late, fail to show up altogether after committing to play, or otherwise let their fellow warriors down. A wise runner of things makes sure such sins have consequences—say, the loss of participation privileges for a while or, if attendance is especially strong and roster spots limited, exile to the back of the queue for the next week's contest.

AWARD GENEROUSLY. We play recreational sports for many reasons, one of which is a desire to imagine we're playing for something other than heart health. So the commissioner needs to act as if the games—and the accomplishments achieved in them—truly matter. Every week I recap the previous Sunday's proceedings, which includes naming an MVP from the winning team. (Often, I take a quick survey immediately after the game; the players like that.) And at the end of each season, I send an awards ballot to league members, on which we vote on numerous categories: MVP, Best Rookie, Most Improved, Most Gentlemanly, etc. Ridiculous? Sure. But everyone takes the time to fill it out.

COMMUNICATE CONSTANTLY. I write e-mails like a frenzied PR flack, a minimum of three a week—more if the weather is bad—to ensure that the game is properly organized (i.e., to guilt players into showing up). I tried using different apps and platforms, but nothing is as efficient as e-mail. There will, unavoidably, be "Reply All" debacles. A wise runner of things will have a fair punishment ready for second offenders.

RECORD RELIGIOUSLY. We keep stats (on Google Docs); mostly TDs, sacks, interceptions, and winning percentages. They mean nothing—at all—and yet . . . the players care. I know this because some of them regularly help me reconcile game data. A few of our players think the numbers are a bad influence—especially when someone intercepts a ball on fourth down that should have been batted away—but I have enough doctors and lawyers, maintenance workers, and students petitioning me to credit them with half a sack to believe the record keeping is a small joy in an otherwise harsh world. Anyway, my career winning percentage is .595, so, you know . . . haters gonna hate.

Continued . . .

DIVERSIFY MEANINGFULLY. Not because it's PC, but because it's a hard-learned fact that groups function better when they are composed of people of differing backgrounds. (Especially if there's a wise runner of things keeping the peace.) In the FDL, that's true in regard to quality of play, but also in regard to camaraderie, morale, decision making, conflict resolution, and—maybe most crucially—participation. Which leads me to my final imperative . . .

RECRUIT MANIACALLY. People retire, get injured, graduate, have kids, and move away, so the commissioner needs to replenish the game's roster constantly. Encourage current players to rope in friends, regardless of skill level. As long as you play six to eight a side, you will always have the playing pieces to configure a pair of competitive teams.

CALL A HORSE RACE

TRAVIS STONE
Announcer, Churchill Downs Racetrack

When I was a kid, I taught myself to call races using toys, marbles, and Matchbox cars; eventually, I graduated to calling ones I watched on TV. If you live near a track, grab a pair of binoculars, find a quiet corner, and announce the races to yourself.

The key to the whole thing is memorizing the jockey silks. Ten minutes before each post time, I walk down to the track with Crayola markers and note the appropriate silk colors next to the horses' names in my program. Then I go through the names, again and again and again, to make the association with the color. I wait another minute and do it one more time. By then, the horses will be headed to the gate. If you haven't matched the silks to the names by then, there's no way you're going to give a good call. People listening to you can always tell if you haven't fully committed the horses to memory. Besides, if you have to look down at your program, you're going to miss the action on the track. That said, sometimes you do forget, and you have to check the program. So I designed a device with a coat hanger and poster board that goes around my neck. My program sits on it like sheet music on a music stand, so I don't have to hold it. That's important because I need my hands free for the binoculars.

As the race unfolds, you have to remember that you're telling its story. Who's first, who's second, who's third, but also who's making a move, who's dropping back, who's speeding up, who's slowing down, who's found trouble. You're responsible for relaying the scene from beginning to end. It's why you really have to love horse racing. You need to understand the thrill and uncertainty so you can convey the drama to the listeners. If you're excited, they will be too.

BET ON GOLF

The second best thing about golf handicaps—a system that measures a golfer's ability (or lack thereof) against an ideal standard—is that they allow players of different skill levels to compete against one another. The first best thing about golf handicaps is that they allow players of different skill levels to *bet* against one another. Friendly wagers make even the most unfulfilling athletic activity enjoyable, and golf is a veritable wellspring of opportunity. Here are a few ways to cash in at the country club.

CLOSE OUT. Here, two teams of two golfers compete in straight-up match play: the lowest combined score (adjusted for handicap) wins the hole. The first team to be ahead by more holes than holes remaining in the round—say, four "up" with three to play—takes the bet. If the bet is settled before the eighteenth tee, you can play the remaining holes for half the original bet to keep things interesting.

NASSAU. The Nassau unwinds in three acts: the front (first nine holes), the back (second nine), and the match (overall outcome). Played by a foursome split into two teams, a $5 Nassau, then, is actually worth $15, with the team winning the most holes (adjusted for handicap) in each portion of the round pocketing the corresponding dough. A common variation doubles the value of the match bet, such as $5 each on the front and back, $10 for the match.

SKINS. This is an individual showdown—and a generally high-stakes one at that—in which each hole awards a predetermined amount to the low shooter (adjusted for handicap). All eighteen "skins" have to be claimed, so when a hole is tied, the bet "carries over" to the next one. In other words, if the first seventeen holes are tied, the final hole is worth eighteen skins.

5-3-1. Also known as "points," this is a threesome classic. Each hole is worth 9 points, with the best score (adjusted for handicap) collecting 5 points, second best 3, and the lagging score 1. In the case of ties, points are divvied up equally, so if two players make par and the other goes one over, the low scorers get 4 points each while Colonel Bogey gets 1. Each "point" is worth a predetermined amount of cash—$1 per is fine—and winnings are determined by end-of-round point differential. Think of it like this: There are 162 points up for grabs (9 x 18 holes), which equals a $54 "commitment" from each member of your threesome. Let's say that by the end of the round, you have 62 points, pal A has 60 points, and pal B has 40. The bottom line is that you're owed $8 (the difference between 62 and 54), pal A is owed $6 (same math, different result), and sad sack pal B has to shell out $14 (the difference between 54 and 40).

JUNK. Also known as "dots," these are pot-sweetening side bets on various scenarios throughout the round. Bets include "sandies" (getting up and down for par out of a sand trap), "greenies" (player closest to the hole on a par 3 makes par), and "birdies" (player takes one fewer stroke than par to finish a hole). Each time a player claims a junk bet, a dot is marked on the scorecard next to his or her score on that hole, and each dot is worth a predetermined amount to be paid out at round's end. In junk bets, handicap adjustments do not apply.

WIN A FACE-OFF

STEVE YZERMAN
NHL Hall of Fame Center

There's no science to it. I tried it all. If something worked, I stuck with it. When it didn't, I changed it up. You're always trying to get as much leverage as possible, and that means cheating when you can. The officials are very strict about the placement of your feet and where you can put your stick blade on the ice, but just before the puck is dropped, you can turn your body to one side or the other to be in the strongest position. So focus on the referee or linesman's hand as he's about to drop the puck. As it gets to that fraction of a second before, move your body into the alignment you want. I was a right-handed shot, so I also flipped my bottom hand from the

standard position (a) so it was on the top of the shaft (b). That gave me more leverage, more strength, to pull the puck back and away from the other guy.

You go into every draw wanting to win it—and with an idea of where you want to win it *to*: where you want to direct the puck. But you have to decide before the puck is dropped what success looks like. In some games you just can't win a face-off—you're having no luck—so you say, "The heck with it, I'm just going to go after his stick and prevent *him* from winning it." Then you tie up his stick and hope one of your wingers comes in and scoops up the puck.

WHERE TO WATCH . . .

A HOCKEY GAME AT THE RINK

Conventional Wisdom: Sit at center ice, halfway up the stands, for a view of the whole game.

For Your Consideration: Take a spot behind one of the goals, as close to the glass as possible. It trades a view of the game as a whole for the more immediate experience of the rough jostling in front of the goal and the tough checks along the boards.

CADDY LIKE A PRO

There's more to being a great caddy than simply schlepping a bag and cleaning equipment. There's also scouting the course, gauging conditions, selecting clubs, tracking balls, and—not least—keeping your golfer grounded. And yet any "looper" will tell you the job boils down to three "ups."

1. **SHOW UP!** This is less a prescription to set your alarm than a command to be fully focused on and committed to the task at hand, mentally and physically. A good caddy is a coach and confidant—by rule, he's the only person the golfer can go to for advice during a round, so a steadfast dedication is essential. Golf is a singular pursuit, but very much a team effort.

2. **KEEP UP!** Never be more than a pace or two behind your golfer and always arrive at the site of the next shot first, ready with answers to all pertinent questions—distance to the green, location of the pin, effect of the wind—before they are posed. Caddies also need to keep up with what's happening elsewhere in the match. Knowing where a golfer stands in relation to the opposition informs the choice between playing it safe and going for broke.

3. **SHUT UP!** Golfers joke that this is the most important "up" of all. Sure, a caddy needs to communicate with his player, but knowing how much (or how little) to say is what keeps you gainfully employed. On pro tours, a feel for what to offer and when to offer it is honed with experience. But a savvy caddy begins any relationship by discussing a golfer's expectations before their first round together, then adjusting his demeanor accordingly as the holes pass.

NOT GET TOSSED FROM A SPORTS VENUE

Judging by the behavior we've all witnessed, one would think there isn't much you could do to warrant a security escort to the exits. Of course, that's not the case. Stadiums and arenas are typically private property, so they have all the rules-setting prerogatives associated with ownership. (Check your ticket's fine print if you're in doubt.) Here's how to keep your nose clean and your butt in your seat.

DON'T

☒ Commit a crime (e.g., assault, harassment, murder).

☒ Get out-of-hand drunk.

☒ Interfere with play, like, say, blowing a whistle to confuse the competitors.

☒ Throw things at players or officials specifically, or on the playing field in general. (Exception: tossing caps onto the rink after a player scores the third goal of a hat trick.)

☒ Trespass on the playing field/rink/court/pitch/track/diamond.

☒ Abscond with a keepsake (i.e., steal something from the building itself, like seats or a piece of equipment).

☒ Get caught scalping tickets (at least in some states; laws vary).*

*For the record, "scalping" in a legal sense refers only to selling tickets above face value, not buying them.

BE A SOLID
FANTASY CITIZEN

———

Fail to follow these four commandments and you might not get invited back to join next year's league.

1. **PAY FULLY AND PROMPTLY.** Do not make the commissioner chase you and your entrance fee.

2. **TAKE YOUR LEAGUE SERIOUSLY . . .** There's nothing more annoying to committed fantasy players than league mates who lose interest. You might think this wouldn't be so (as every quitter means one fewer person trying to win money), but you'd be wrong (since every quitter offers everyone else a shot at an easy W or a ridiculously one-sided trade). If you commit, stay committed.

3. **. . . BUT NOT TOO SERIOUSLY.** Even if you're playing for an obscene amount of money, try to remember that you're playing a game. Trash talk and bragging are fine—expected, really. Nastiness and underhandedness are not. There's no clearer signal that you're not to be trusted than dissing a player—with real malice—behind his back to another.

4 **DO UNTO OWNERS AS YOU WOULD HAVE THEM DO UNTO YOU.** Don't send out a trade offer that lowballs your rival. It's insulting. Proper etiquette requires that you contact her first to gauge interest. Then let the negotiations begin.

PRESIDENTS AND PASSERS

THE QUESTION

Only four of the four thousand colleges or universities in the United States have produced both a president and a Super Bowl-winning quarterback. Can you name them?

THE ANSWER

1. Miami University in Ohio (Benjamin Harrison, 23rd president; Ben Roethlisberger, Steelers, SB XL, XLIII)

2. Stanford University (Herbert Hoover, 31st president; Jim Plunkett, Raiders, SB XV, XVIII; John Elway, Broncos, SB XXXII, XXXIII)

3. University of Michigan (Gerald Ford, 38th president; Tom Brady, Patriots, SB XXXVI, XXXVIII, XLIX)

4. United States Naval Academy (Jimmy Carter, 39th president; Roger Staubach, Cowboys, SB VI, XII)

ROLL A STRIKE

ROD ROSS
Head Coach, U.S. National Bowling Team

Going straight at the lead pin results in more splits than strikes. You want to come in from the side. But a bowling lane is more than eighteen times longer than it is wide. To get the ball to come in at the right angle, you need to hook or curve it a little bit over a long way (see opposite). The problem is, hooks are almost impossible to throw at your average bowling center. Bowling lanes are often oiled to protect them from the hard objects thrown on them. And because house balls are made to last, they aren't designed with much traction. When they hit the oil, they slide, and that means they go straight. You can try manipulating them into a hook by not using your thumb, or by twisting them to give them some English (aka spin), but that's very hard to control. If you bowl regularly—even a few times a year—it's worth buying your own ball.

That said, there are things you can do with a house ball to increase your chance of a strike. Let's start with the size of the ball. It should be heavy enough to swing your arm, not the other way around. If you can hold it at the top of your backswing, it's too light. But if it pulls you around on your backswing, it's too heavy. Generally, women should choose a ball between 10 and 14 pounds; guys between 13 and 15.

Your grip matters too. Most amateurs pick up a ball by putting their fingers and thumb in the holes at the same time. But if you do that, they come out at the same time when you throw too, and that creates control problems. Instead, pick up the ball from the ball return with your fingers and thumb in the holes, then take them out and turn the ball over so the holes

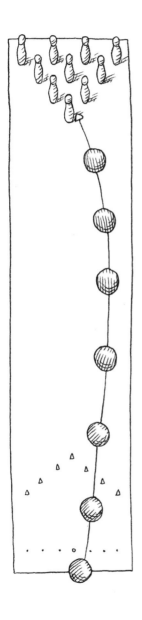

are on the bottom. Then put your fingers in the ball from underneath, thumb last. Now when you release the ball, everything is reversed: The ball will roll off your thumb, onto your palm, and your fingers will come out last. And that allows you to control the direction.

For the approach, you should be on the balls of your feet, knees slightly flexed, ball waist high or above in front of you, hand relaxed. There's a big dot in the middle of the lane. Start about one dot (if you are wide shouldered) or two (if you are narrow shouldered) to the right of that middle dot if you're right-handed, or to the left if you're left-handed. Footwork is another place where people have trouble because it's the opposite of a normal gait. When you walk down the street, as your left foot goes forward, your right arm goes forward, and vice versa. To reach a proper finish in bowling, though—left foot sliding, right hand releasing the ball—you have to start off balance. Begin with your right foot *and* right arm going forward, or the reverse if you're left-handed. After that first step, you'll be in synch. Well, after a lot of practice.

HOST A TAILGATE

PAUL VALETUTTI JR.
Member, New York Giants Tailgate D2

Everyone does burgers and hot dogs, so for the love of Refrigerator Perry, go a different way. We often serve something from the regional cuisine of the opposing team: say, gumbo when the Saints are in town. Our motto is "Eat 'em and beat 'em." But the right food is only one piece of the puzzle.

PLAN YOUR MENU by Wednesday or Thursday of game week, at the latest. Write it down.

PREP FOOD on Friday and Saturday, leaving Sunday morning free so you can get to the stadium as early as possible.

DON'T FORGET FOLDING TABLES AND CHAIRS, plus plastic utensils and paper goods, oven mitts, garbage bags (recycling too), and disposable aluminum pans, which will make your life much easier come cleanup time.

SET UP TWO SEPARATE STATIONS: one for cooking, another for serving.

ENJOY A CEREMONIAL FIRST BEER. Pair it with a ceremonial first toss of the pigskin. Savor the moment. It might be the most satisfying one of the day.

THINK OF BEER AS THE TAILGATER'S CHICKEN STOCK; you can use it to keep whatever you're cooking from drying out. A citrusy beer works wonders in a stew or pulled pork.

HAVE A HOSPITALITY POLICY. If you've followed the plan correctly, hungry strangers will be stopping by. You have to decide if you want to serve them. I sometimes put out a piggy bank and ask that before visitors grab a plate they throw in whatever amount they want to help offset the cost. Most people are more than willing to chip in.

BE A BATKID

Few toil in such anonymity on so public a stage as the batboys and batgirls of Major League Baseball. But someone has to pick up the bats, muddy the balls, clean the cleats, and wipe the helmets of the Boys of Summer. So why not you? There's really only one reason: you're not yet fourteen years old, MLB's age of majority since 2002, when a three-year-old batboy—son of Giants manager Dusty Baker—was nearly bowled over during a play at home plate.

Of course, it helps to be physically fit, diplomatic in dealing with the wildly varying personalities of world-class athletes, and able to keep up with your schoolwork despite a gig that keeps you busy until midnight. However, don't consider the job if you're trying to see America. Most batkids don't travel with their teams; instead, they staff both dugouts at the home park. And don't sign up if you're looking to get rich: If you get paid at all—in many cities it's a volunteer gig—it will be no more than minimum wage. Then again, can you really put a price tag on a bucket-list, swag-filled experience?

In any case, landing one of these coveted positions may come down to whether you know someone in the organization. But some teams—in both the major and minor leagues—hold open job tryouts before each season. A phone call or an e-mail to a team's community relations or media department is the quickest way to find out the schedule. Know, though, that waiting lists for consideration are often quite long. In other words, reach out now.

AT THE GYM

Because "that guy" is a walking, talking health code violation.

DO	DON'T
Leave the locker room a little cleaner than when you got there.	Leave used towels and other detritus for the maintenance staff to pick up. Find the right bin and use it.
Use your towel to wipe off whatever equipment you've just used.	Hang that towel on a neighboring machine or bench as you use another.
Return all barbells, kettlebells, and other free weights and equipment once you're done with them.	Block access to the dumbbell rack while you work out in front of the mirror.
Grunt, if you must, but show some restraint.	Talk to people wearing headphones or earbuds unless you have a specific purpose that's not a come-on.
Ask unoccupied individuals—staff or patrons—for spotting help or advice about technique.	Interrupt someone else's session with a "quick question" for their trainer.
Bring a water bottle with you as you make your circuit.	Bring a coat or gym bag with you as you make your circuit. Leave those items in a locker.
Take no more than two long draws at the drinking fountain if there are people waiting in line behind you.	Spit in the fountain. Ever. (Should we really have to tell you that?!)

FIELD A GROUNDER

OMAR VIZQUEL
Retired MLB Shortstop

Everyone talks about how good your hands have to be, but no one talks about feet. And the secret is where your feet are. They should be parallel to each other, set a little wider than your shoulders. If they're too far apart or too close together, you won't be balanced, and that will make it harder to field the ball cleanly or throw it afterward. Before the ball is hit, you have to be ready for anything; you may need to move in any direction. That's why you should be bending your knees a bit by the time the pitch crosses the plate, so you're ready to take off. You can't be flat-footed either; you need to be on your toes (a).

No matter which way you have to go, the most important thing is to remember to keep moving, to be fluid. That is, don't stop hard, because then you won't be able to change direction for a bad hop. Ideally, you should be in position to field the ball with both hands, with your glove hand lower, the web near or on the ground, and your throwing hand a little higher, open and ready to reach in and grab the ball once it's inside the glove (b). Always watch the ball all the way into the glove. And think of the ball as an egg you don't want to break—absorb it more than catch it—cradling it from the ground up into your stomach, down and up in a circular movement, to soften the impact. I also tell young guys to treat the ball like their girlfriend: delicately. Only after you field it should you look to the base you have to throw to. Sometimes you have to throw off-balance, like when there's a fast runner and you have to get rid of the ball quickly. But there's an old saying: Nobody is faster than the ball. So don't rush if you don't have to; take the time to get set and make a balanced throw. And remember your feet.

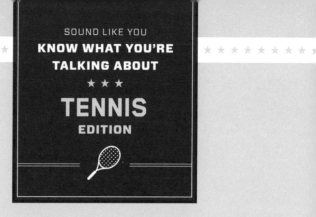

SOUND LIKE YOU
**KNOW WHAT YOU'RE
TALKING ABOUT**

★ ★ ★

TENNIS
EDITION

THREE TOPICS UP FOR DISCUSSION

1 PAY PARITY

As a rule, prize purses for female players remain less than those offered the men. Per another rule, when the guys in the sport are forced to speak to the issue, they often put their tennis shoes in their mouths.

2 MATCH FIXING

A slow drip of scandals suggests that more than a few players have given less than their best at the behest of unsavory crime rings. To date, allegation has far outpaced indictment, but this is an individual sport (the outcomes of which are easier to manipulate than those in team competitions) that attracts lots of betting (second only to soccer internationally), so the preconditions for trouble are worrisome.

3 DOPING

Like most sports, tennis struggles to ensure that its athletes aren't enhancing their games with illegal drugs. Unlike most sports, tennis lost a marquee name in 2016 when Maria Sharapova was suspended for fifteen months after testing positive. It is the most severe punishment levied by a governing body often accused of protecting its image at all costs. Some say it heralds a new era of accountability. Others think it's simply a case of throwing an aging star to the wolves.

WHAT TO SAY WHEN . . .

. . . THE HAWK-EYE SYSTEM IS EMPLOYED TO JUDGE A CLOSE LINE CALL:
"I miss John McEnroe."

. . . TWO MALE PLAYERS RALLY FOR MORE THAN A FEW STROKES:
"I miss wood rackets."

. . . SOMEONE MENTIONS THE AUSTRALIAN OPEN:
"Is it really a 'major' if no one knows who won until the next day?"

WHEN IN DOUBT, BRING UP . . .

ROGER FEDERER AND STEFFI GRAF

No man has spent more weeks ranked number 1 in the world than the current star has.

No human has spent more time as the number 1 player in the world than she did (in the 1980s and '90s).

SAMPLE CHATTER:
"If Roger Federer were any better, he'd be Steffi Graf."

Continued . . .

ONE DEBATE YOU CAN WIN

Should male and female players play the same number of sets in Grand Slam matches?

THE PREMISE

Female players are required to win two of three sets, while their male counterparts must take three of five.

YOUR POSITION
Why in the world not?

YOUR ARGUMENT

Is the women's mile in track and field shorter than the men's? Better yet, is the marathon fewer miles? This quaint tennis practice is a vestige of a time when women were thought to be more fragile than men. Suffice it to say that shorter matches rob fans of the high drama of the five-setter. Women at the WTA championships and other tournaments are already handling the best-of-five format just fine.

A FEW FEARLESS FORECASTS TO MAKE

DEFINITELY!

A woman or a man will once again achieve a calendar-year singles Grand Slam (for the first time since 1988 for women, and 1969 for men).

POSSIBLY . . .

The international team competition known as the Davis Cup will end, because even most tennis fans don't know it exists.

WHY NOT?

Women's purses will be bigger than men's—because the women's game is more fun to watch.

Fun Fact to Impress Your Friends

Tennis's weird scoring system—you need four points to win a game, but the points are 15, 30, 40, and victory—is less strange if you think of a single game as a trip around a clock face (which is in itself a strange way to think about it, except that some people believe that early lawn tennis games were in fact scored on clock faces). So one can imagine the first point being "marked" at the "3" (i.e., 15 minutes past); the second point at the "6" (i.e., 30 minutes past); and the third at . . . yeah, that's a problem. But even the fact that the third point is 40—not 45—makes some sense: Sticking with the clock face, consider that to win a game, one must beat an opponent by two points, which in the case of a tie after the third point requires "splitting" the remaining fifteen minutes. Thing is, it's easier to halve 20 than 15, so if the third point is 40, an advantage to one player would be easily represented by putting a clock hand halfway between the "8" and "12" (i.e., at the "10").

Once you clear that up for the crowd, you'll doubtless be asked to explain why a score of zero is known as "love." In the game's early days, French players, thinking the numeral "0" resembled an egg, called out "egg" in their native language: *l'oeuf*. Say "*l'oeuf*" to an Englishman often enough and it starts to sound like "love." Interestingly, the French no longer call a zero an "egg." They call it *zéro*.

PICK A UNIFORM NUMBER

To be clear, we are addressing athletes here. Or parents of athletes. (If you are a grown adult considering the purchase of a replica team jersey for personal use beyond Halloween or bedtime, see page 253.) Just because athletes at whatever level can pretty much choose any available number they want doesn't mean they should. Please keep in mind these five rules.

RULE #1: BE RESPECTFUL. Be careful when choosing a number that's inextricably linked to one player—for example, 99 and Wayne Gretzky. Your play, not a unique number, needs to reveal your greatness. That said, it's okay to pay historical homage, such as "I wear 24 because of Willie Mays—the best center fielder of all time. Period." Context, implied or explained, is crucial.

RULE #2: BE DISCERNING. Choosing to honor a lesser-known athlete is acceptable, even laudable. But you'll really impress friends if that player happens to be a low-potential grinder.

RULE #3: BE HUMBLE. Some sports have rules that govern the numbers for certain positions, such as 1 through 19 for football quarterbacks. Others just rely on age-worn customs to maintain order. Stick to them. Again, talent should be what draws attention.

RULE #4: BE SELF-AWARE. Speaking of people staring at you: Some numbers just look better on tall or lanky athletes (7 or 11, for example), while others are more obviously suited for stockier body types (56 or 00). If you're not sure about your numeral feng shui, ask someone you trust.

RULE #5: BE RATIONAL. There are no lucky (or unlucky) numbers, only superstitious athletes. The list of legends who wore 13, for example, includes Wilt Chamberlain, Dan Marino, and Alex Rodriguez.

WEAR A FOAM FINGER

DON'T.*

---

*Not if you're older than, say, twelve. You'll look like a dork, and brandishing one will most certainly block someone else's view.

BLOCK A SHOT

ANGELA RUGGIERO
Former Defenseman, U.S. Women's National Ice Hockey Team

First you have to decide if you should make the attempt. If the player you're responsible for is winding up, then certainly you want to get in front of the puck. But if it's not your player, blocking the shot is not your primary role in the defensive scheme.

If you are defending the puck, focus on positioning and making yourself look as big as possible. For starters, don't stand straight in front of the shooter with your two skates on the ice because the puck is going to go right by you. Besides, blocking pucks with ankles or skates—which is what you'd be doing in that situation if you were lucky enough to get a piece of the shot—really hurts. Also, never line yourself up with the body of the shooter; line up with the puck instead. Personally, diving into the puck as a shooter winds up is one of my favorite things to do. It's basically a slide tackle, like a soccer goalie would make. Men don't try this one too much because their faces aren't protected by visors like ours are. Keep in mind, though, that you can end up looking foolish if the shooter fakes and you end up sprawled on the ice. So don't leave your feet until the shooter's stick begins its downswing.

The best blocking position is a half pose (see opposite). Down on one knee, leg flared out, your upper body creating a box—arms at your sides, chest up. That puts you square to the shooter, with your torso perpendicular to the puck, and you look big, both up high and down low. As a rule, a shooter's best chance to score is keeping the puck low, but that means it has the best chance of hitting you too—hopefully in your shin pad. The half pose is

the way to go because if the shooter fakes a shot and begins to skate around you, you can quickly stand up and defend again. Similarly, if you do redirect the puck, you can get back in the play quickly. If you've left both skates, though—either sliding or going down to both knees—it's much harder to get up to chase. Then again, if you're killing a penalty and the shooter is at the dot or top of the circle, all bets are off. Slide!

INSURE AN ATHLETIC CAREER

Most fans have come across reports of athletes insuring their arm (MLB pitcher Clayton Kershaw), legs (soccer legend David Beckham), and other moneymaking body parts. But while such stories are excellent fodder for sports bar conversation, they're not usually accurate. What these athletes are actually insuring is their ability to earn money in their specific sport with their particular talent against any and all manner of calamity. Yes, that would cover losing a pitching arm in a freak logging accident, but it might also include losing the ability to pitch with that arm because of an energy-sapping autoimmune disease.

Such policies generally come under the heading of "surplus lines," so called because the coverage sought would be declined by some carriers because of its size or the irregular nature of the risk. Cost varies with the sport, the athlete's age, and the duration of risk, but for a college football player, say, the premium on $1 million of permanent total disability coverage and a $1 million "loss of value" rider (see chart, opposite) would be around $11,000.

"SURPLUS LINES" INSURANCE FOR ATHLETES

TYPE	WHAT IT COVERS
Draft Protection	Athlete-owned policy covering permanent loss of value from total disability, or an injury that doesn't keep the athlete from playing but lowers his earning power due to later-than-predicted draft selection.
Temporary Disability Protection	Athlete-owned policy, targeting big-draw athletes. But athletes who don't compete in team sports—golfers, racecar drivers, tennis players—may also purchase similar coverage.
Loss of Value *(Future Contract Value)*	Athlete-owned policy, often bought in the final year of a pro contract—or before a final college season—to protect against loss of projected income due to injury or illness. May also be used as protection for falling in the draft for reasons other than injury.
Contract Guarantee	Team-owned policy that offsets salary payments to permanently or temporarily disabled athletes with guaranteed contracts.
Permanent Total Disability	Team-owned policy that covers a career-ending illness or injury.
Accidental Death	Athlete- or team-owned policy covering death unrelated to sickness.

GET ON TV AT A SPORTING EVENT

If you're reading this entry, you have come to grips with the fact that the most direct way to accomplish this feat—to be a good enough athlete to take the field—will forever elude you. (Good for you; self-delusion is a killer.) Luckily, all is not lost. You can still score some screen time if you . . .

THINK LIKE A PRODUCER. Watch a few broadcasts of the sport in which you intend to make your appearance, ideally by the network that will be airing the game you plan to attend. Field producers and networks have their own preferred angles, images, and storytelling patterns.

THINK LIKE A CAMERA OPERATOR. Or more precisely, think like a camera*man*, because most of the ten to twenty operators at a typical network game will be male. For better or worse, that means they're likely to be attracted to photogenic women. Be such a photogenic woman—or the guy sitting between two of them.

THINK LIKE A CENSOR. Streaking or causing some other interruption of play is a waste of time. Not only will it get you thrown out of the venue—and possibly arrested—but most broadcasters long ago stopped offering airtime to such hijinks. Likewise, avoid controversy-causing costumes, such as religious figures holding footballs or political cutouts. Members of the TV crew aren't likely to jeopardize their jobs for the shock value.

PAINT YOUR FACE. For mysterious reasons, camera operators are still mildly amused by those who use their skin as a canvas, especially those who do so in groups.

USE YOUR WORDS. Signs with clearly drawn block letters are most likely to get noticed (and approved for airing by producers).

BE CREATIVE—OR CRAVEN. The signs you make should (1) tell a quick story; (2) refer to a recent, noncontroversial event or player in the game; or (3) give a shout-out to the network or on-air employees thereof.

SHOW UP EARLY. Many of the fan shots you see during lulls were actually taken before the game started, because TV folk don't like to be the cause of blocked views.

SIT AS CLOSE AS YOU CAN. Rarely is a shot taken of the upper deck. (Exception: if you're the *only* fan in a very large and distant section, especially if you follow the advice above. Or are sound asleep.)

TAKE A SPORTS PHOTO

ANDREW D. BERNSTEIN
Director of Photography, Staples Center

I've been shooting the Dodgers for ten years, the Lakers for more than thirty. They have their strategies and I have mine.

ON THE CAMERA: Tailor your equipment to the sport. If you're shooting soccer, or something else from a long distance, you need a different lens than if your subject is baseball or even Pop Warner football, where you can get closer to the action. Most brands sell cameras with a couple of lenses that cover a broad focal range.

ON RANGE: My rule of thumb is: Get in tight. The tighter you are, the more interesting the photo. Think about it. There's a guy at the plate. Do you want him and half of the crowd in the photo, or do you want a close-up of the guy as the ball hits his bat? There are definitely times you want the wide shot to tell the story, but usually I get as close as I can.

ON TIMING: You have to anticipate the action. If you're late, you won't get the ball on the foot, the bat on the ball, the ball leaving the hand. It takes practice. Never take your eye from the camera. If you actually see it happen, it means you missed the photo. During Kobe Bryant's final game, I didn't take my eye from the camera for a second. Literally. I would have missed something critical, and I'd be kicking myself for the rest of my career.

ON FOCUS: If the eyes of the subject are in focus, your photo should be. For longer shots, all of today's cameras have autofocus, which makes life a lot easier.

ON PERSPECTIVE: I like candid portraits, where you're not shooting action but trying to get the feeling of the game—through people's faces, dirty shoes, or a ripped glove, any of the small elements that tell the story of the athlete, the game, or the sport itself.

WHERE TO WATCH . . .

A TENNIS MATCH AT THE COURT

Conventional Wisdom: Sit behind a baseline, one-third to one-half of the way up the stands. From there, the perspective allows for an accurate read of the ball's trajectory, you get a chance to be close to both players over the course of the match, and, best of all, you won't leave with a sore neck from following all those back-and-forth rallies.

For Your Consideration: Get super low (behind the baseline) for at least part of the match, if you can wrangle it. There's no better vantage point from which to appreciate the power and speed of the game at its highest level.

WIN AT H-O-R-S-E

You know the game: A player calls her shot. If the basket is made, the opponent must match it or he earns a letter. Spell the word and you lose. Obviously, those with the more polished touch stand a better chance of winning. But most of us aren't exactly Steph Curry, so stop thinking NBA and start thinking Harlem Globetrotter. A trick shot or two will surprise your foe and keep you in control.* Here are three reasonably easy-to-master options.

1. SEAT-OF-THE-PANTS SLING

Park your butt on the court behind the foul line, and let the ball fly. It seems simple, but it's way harder than it looks. And that's why it's perfect.

2. RICK BARRY'S REVENGE

The NBA star was one of the few pros of the modern game to use an underhanded motion for free throws. Other basketball players see it as childlike and embarrassing, but it's actually far more accurate; Barry, who's in the Hall of Fame, has one of the highest career free-throw percentages in NBA history. If it's good enough for him, it's good enough for H-O-R-S-E. And you can get good enough at it quickly.

3. BACKWARD BLIND BALLOON BALL

Stand at the top of the key with your back to the hoop. Lean back to get a good view, then straighten and use an underhanded, over-the-head motion with both arms to float the ball with a high arc against the backboard and in. (You can try to swish it, but the backboard is more forgiving of errors of force and trajectory.)

---

*The Code of the Court: It's lame to keep repeating a shot that's working if you're just playing for fun, but it's totally legit if there's money on the line.

Seat-of-the-Pants Sling

Rick Barry's Revenge

Backward Blind Balloon Ball

GET DRAFTED

If you can survive the paperwork, scout scrutiny, league vetting, and predraft workouts, you may wind up on a Big 4 team's board come draft day. That is, if you meet the basic qualifications for being "draft eligible," which vary a good deal from league to league.

NBA

- During the calendar year of the draft, players must be at least nineteen years of age, and at least one year removed from the graduation of their high school class.
- In addition, one of a host of other requirements must be met. The two most relevant:
    - Player has exhausted four years of college eligibility—that is, the four seasons an incoming freshman can be expected to play.
    - Player has been released from a contract with a team outside the NBA.
- Players from other countries are automatically eligible in the calendar year they turn twenty-two; younger players may seek early entry.

Note: The NCAA allows collegiate players to declare as often as they like without losing their remaining eligibility, as long as they remove their name from consideration before the draft deadline.

NHL

- Players must be age eighteen or older, except in certain situations included in the College Bargaining Agreement.

NFL

- Players must be at least three years removed from high school.
- All college football eligibility must be used before the start of the next season, but underclassmen and players who have graduated before using all their eligibility may request league approval to enter the draft early.
- Players qualify only in the year after the end of their eligibility.
- Players whose eligibility has changed since the most recent draft may be selected in a supplemental draft. (However, a player may not simply choose to bypass the NFL draft to be eligible for the supplemental draft.)

MLB

- Players must reside in the United States, Puerto Rico or other U.S. territories, or Canada, or be enrolled in a U.S. high school or college.
- High school players qualify only if they have graduated and have not attended college or junior college.
- Junior college players qualify no matter how many years they've completed.
- College players qualify only if they have completed their junior or senior years or are at least twenty-one years old.
- Residents of the United States and Canada must never have signed a major or minor league contract.

EXECUTE A HIGH FIVE

Legend has it that Glenn Burke, an outfielder for the Los Angeles Dodgers, invented the high five on the final day of the 1977 season, after teammate Dusty Baker hit his thirtieth home run of the year. Burke, who was next up, held his right hand high above his head after Baker crossed home plate, and Baker responded by reaching up and smacking it. But that's only chapter one of the story: In his at-bat, Burke also hit a home run, the first of his Major League career, and when he got back to the dugout, Baker raised his hand to reciprocate the salute. Thus a tradition was born, soon to be adopted worldwide by both professional and amateur athletes, not to mention everyone else with something to celebrate or congratulations to bestow.

There are right and wrong ways to deliver a high five. If we're being honest, all of us have misfired on the maneuver, resulting in embarrassment for both sides. But it need never be so again. One guiding principle will guarantee success in all future hand-smack endeavors: Look at the other person's elbow (see below).

That's it. It may seem counterintuitive to stare at something other than the target, and we can't explain why it works. But it does work. Every time.

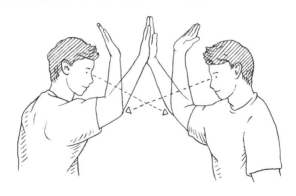

ICE AN INJURY

When we get physical, we get hurt, which is why God invented ice. (Well, for that and cocktails.) But not every tweak and twinge will benefit from the cold embrace of the ice pack. Chronic conditions like bad backs? Not so much. (Try heat treatment.) Serendipitous sprains, strains, and swelling? You bet. So if that's what ails you, administer thusly.

1. **GET ICE** in a form that can mold around the relevant body part, such as shavings, pellets, or small cubes.

2. **APPLY ICE** with a waterproof bag held in place with an elastic bandage.

3. **REMOVE ICE** after no more than twenty minutes, to avoid freezer burn.

4. **APPLY ICE AGAIN** when body temperature gets back to normal, for another twenty minutes.

5. **REPEAT CYCLE** three times in the twelve hours after the injury.

BLOCK SOMEONE WHO'S BIGGER THAN YOU ARE

TOMMIE ROBINSON
College Football Coach

Defensive players get a running start, which generates lots of momentum. So technique is critical. If you're not technically sound, you won't have a chance. Quickness—exploding off the ball as the play begins—is especially important, because it cuts the distance the defender has to build momentum. We teach that the block should occur on the defensive side of the line of scrimmage, not ours, because it allows you to establish your point before the defensive player establishes his. After you close the distance, though, you have to stop. You can't just run into the other guy. Instead, you're looking to leverage him, and that begins with setting a solid base.

Your feet should be armpit- to shoulder-width apart, and they shouldn't come together at any point during the block. Bend your knees to keep your shoulders below his; that's also crucial. And pay attention to where you put your head. If the play is going outside, your head has to be outside the defender. If the play is going inside, your head needs to be inside too. Now, explode your hips into the contact, thrusting all the power of your legs through your whole body to stop his charge. At the same time, shoot out your hands. Don't just lay them on the defender—be violent with them. Make sure your wrists are higher than your elbows and your thumbs are pointing up. If you're lower than the defender, you should be able to shoot those thumbs at the inside edges of his chest plate. Even if you miss the exact area, shooting your hands will stop some momentum.

Of course, there's another option: you can cut him, go for his knees. It sounds dirty, but sometimes you just have to even things out. Bud Casey, whom I coached with at TCU, used to say, "I don't care how big they are. Everybody's knees weigh the same." Cutting is about sending a message. Once you start worrying about getting cut, you don't come in so fast, and that gives the smaller player a chance.

WHERE TO WATCH . . .

A FOOTBALL GAME AT THE STADIUM

Conventional Wisdom: Head straight to the 50-yard line, halfway up. A spot there offers angles that most closely approximate the ones you experience on your TV at home. Don't sit too close to ground level; you'll miss a lot of action as you try to see past the backs of the very large uniformed men standing on the sideline. Either way, pack binoculars. Things at the fringes of a 100-yard rectangle are smaller than they appear.

For Your Consideration: Sit behind one of the end zones for a perspective like no other. It's kind of like watching an invading army (coming or going).

BET THE HORSES

A day at the track is an essential fan-going experience, but most of that experience is about the wagering. That said, horse racing is called "the sport of kings" for a reason—unless you're in charge of your country's exchequer, you need to be prudent. Our advice: Pack a stack you're okay to lose and don't go back to the ATM if you do lose it. You'd best bring a working knowledge of how to play the ponies too. For starters, when you get to the betting window, know the race number, the program number of the horse you're backing, the amount of your bet, and the type of bet you want to make. You may need to announce the track of the race you're betting too, as many venues offer opportunities to follow the action at faraway tracks. Etiquette demands that you have money in hand; anyone fumbling for his wallet as post time approaches is not looked at kindly by those standing behind him in line. Of course, all of that only allows you to *look* like you know what you're doing. You'll need to get to know these primary gambling options to ensure that those looks don't deceive.

WIN. You're betting the horse finishes first. If you're right, you collect at the posted odds (that is, the odds set by the track and the subsequent betting action).

PLACE. You're betting the horse finishes first *or* second. The payoff odds are slightly lower.

SHOW. You're betting the horse finishes first *or* second *or* third. The payout is accordingly minimal.

ACROSS THE BOARD. You're essentially making three bets on a single horse—to win, place, and show. So a $2 across-the-board bet runs you $6. If your horse places or shows, you collect at the posted odds for that outcome—and if the horse wins, you collect on all three.

EXACTA. You're betting two horses finish first and second in a particular order, as in number 7 will win and number 5 will place. It pays out at higher odds than betting each separately, but that's because picking two horses to finish in front is twice as hard as picking one. You can also "box" this bet, meaning you'll win either way as long as they finish one-two, but this is considered two bets so it will cost you double.

QUINELLA. You're betting two horses finish first and second, in either order. It's just one bet so it's less expensive and less remunerating than an exacta box.

TRIFECTA. You're betting three horses to win, place, and show in an exact order. Here's your biggest chance for an extravagant payday, particularly if a long shot or two finishes in the money. A boxed trifecta (meaning the three horses you've chosen can win, place, and show in any order) will cost you six times as much, but tracks take $1 trifecta wagers.

SUPERFECTA. You're betting four horses to win, place, show, and come in fourth in an exact order. Good luck with that.

MINISTER TO ATHLETES

Athletes are as spiritually minded as the rest of us—if not more so—which at least partly explains why they so often invoke a higher power in postgame interviews. Not surprisingly, most professional teams have a relationship—typically informal—with at least one pastor-type or association of clergy folk. Looking for insight into the soul-saving business, we interviewed Steve Sisco of the Baseball Chapel, which tends to the incorporeal needs of hundreds of major and minor league ballplayers.

Q: You refer to yourselves as chapel leaders, not chaplains. What's the difference?

A: We function more like a church for the players, rather than simply a chaplain or counselor. We have pastors who minister just as they would in a regular place of worship, but we also offer prayer services, as well as one-on-one studies, marriage counseling, grief counseling, and those kinds of things.

Q: Do you minister to athletes of all faiths?

A: Athletes usually seek out leaders in their own faith. But everyone, of course, is welcome.

Q: Who makes up your congregation?

A: The whole world of professional baseball: players and their families, front office personnel, even stadium personnel—from security guards to ushers to clubhouse managers to anyone in operations.

Q: What do players need from you?

A: Baseball is a game of failure. Hitters who fail 70 percent of the time are All-Stars. It's important for them to have their head right. They may seem to have it all, but they hurt, celebrate, and mourn like the rest of us.

Q: Do you seek out players who may have issues?

A: No. We build relationships, so the players allow us into their lives. Once that happens, then we may initiate conversations.

Q: What kinds of issues come up?

A: Being on the road for almost half the year, a lot of family issues arise—husband and wife stuff or father and kids. We have women's ministry leaders who minister to players' wives.

Q: What is the chapel's connection to MLB?

A: We are guests in the stadium, with no official relationship with the league beyond their ongoing invitation to minister to the players. All of our funding comes from the players.

Q: Are chapel leaders paid?

A: No, they're not, but their expenses are. All of them have jobs outside of what they do for us. Most have freedom: the church gives them time to serve with us.

Q: Have players ever given you advice?

A: Their advice is to be more cultural than spiritual. We're like missionaries in a foreign country. We don't want to "westernize" them; we want to understand their culture so we can communicate with them. The players are aware that most of our guys are outsiders, though, so they help them get acclimated.

Q: What's the toughest moment in a player's career you need to deal with?

A: For me, as a former player, it was relinquishing the game. As I minister to those who are approaching the end of their careers, I know it weighs heavily on everybody, whether they come to chapel or not.

THROW A SOFTBALL DROP PITCH

It doesn't matter if you pitch in a beer league, for a Sunday-morning men's club, or for something more official, a drop is a must-have weapon in any softball hurler's arsenal, the third-pitch complement to that fastball-changeup combo. Here's how to bring it.

1. Grip the ball as you would a four-seam fastball, with fingertips along the "horseshoe" side of the stitching.

2. Use a regular windmill windup, but with a more compact stride—maybe a foot shorter. Come through with your weight on the stride foot (the one opposite your pitching arm) while keeping your shoulders above your hips. Do *not* bend at the waist.

3. At the release point, relax your shoulders and keep your elbow close to your body, with your wrist pointed at the catcher.

4. Now the tricky part, which is best imagined as the motion a magician makes to pull a tablecloth out from under a place setting. As you release the ball, pull back and slightly up with your fingertips, to maximize the spin, as you lift off your back leg and put more weight on your front.

CONGRATULATIONS!
YOU THREW A DROP PITCH.

Except, you know, probably not at first. As with all things, learning the drop takes work. And because the timing of the release must be precise, it's helpful to learn it at a slower speed than a regular fastball. Over time you'll be able to increase velocity—and with it the number of your strikeout victims.

TELL A SPORTS STORY

Everybody enjoys a good reminiscence—as long as it's artfully recounted.

IF YOU WITNESSED IT . . .

DON'T BE A ONE-UPPER. Wait a few minutes before following someone else's Super Bowl halftime show saga with your Super Bowl tailgate saga.

ALWAYS PROVIDE CONTEXT. All your friends from St. Louis will know what you mean when you refer to the Blues' come-from-behind victory over the Flames in Game 6 of the 1986 Western Conference semifinals as the "Monday Night Miracle" . . . but almost assuredly no one else in the Western Hemisphere will.

DON'T BE A GAME-DROPPER. There better be a very specific reason you're referencing your attendance at a high-profile event. Otherwise, your audience will figure you're bringing it up just to show off.

DON'T RUB IT IN. A fan of the losing side *really* doesn't want to hear how much fun you had in the stands while their team was getting crushed.

IF YOU ACTUALLY DID IT . . .

BE SELF-AWARE. Unless the setting is major college or above, any tale of personal prowess should start with a clear acknowledgment of your (relatively low) standing in the athletic firmament.

BE SELF-DEPRECATING. Often, the best recollections of physical accomplishment include at least one moment of klutzy behavior, abject fear, or poor decision making.

BE ON POINT. The play you made to win it all might very well be interesting, but the backstory of your teammate's heroic fight with scurvy is almost certainly not.

BE BRIEF. You enjoy reliving every detail, but most storytelling showcases limit performers to seven or eight minutes for a reason. Limit yourself to three. Tell it right, though, and maybe you'll get to answer questions afterward.

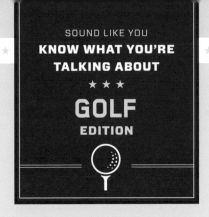

THREE TOPICS UP FOR DISCUSSION

1 TIGER'S SHADOW

While the sport thrives, it longs for the must-watch appeal of Tiger Woods, who's been hampered by injuries and age (plus a very public dissolution of his marriage that will never fade from memory). That people continue to expect a full comeback both proves his impact and distracts from appreciating the most varied bunch of talented players ever.

2 THE SEOUL OF THE WOMEN'S GAME

The LPGA has for years been dominated by Korean golfers, which some observers worry has limited the sport's appeal to U.S. audiences.

3 WANING PARTICIPATION

Although people still watch major tournaments, fewer kids are picking up the game and many courses are closing. This may have something to do with the time and expense required to play.

WHAT TO SAY WHEN . . .

. . . MENTION IS MADE OF OLYMPIC GOLF:

"Can anyone explain to me why golf is back in the Olympics?"

. . . SOMEONE QUESTIONS WHETHER GOLF IS A SPORT:

"It's in the Olympics, isn't it?"

. . . A PRO MISSES A SHORT PUTT:

"He's better when there's a windmill between him and the hole."

. . . A BROADCASTER REFERS TO THE MASTERS AS "A TRADITION LIKE NO OTHER":

"And that tradition is . . . really ugly jackets!"

FOUR HOLES (AND COURSES) THAT MATTER

1 HOLE 18 AT PEBBLE BEACH

This right-to-left dogleg par-5 on the Pacific Ocean is considered the most spectacular finishing hole in the sport.

2 HOLE 17 AT ST. ANDREWS (OLD COURSE)

Known affectionately as the Road Hole, this tricky par-4 is famous for ruining British Open scores. It helps that it's located on the Scottish course considered to be the Jerusalem *and* Mecca of the sport.

3 HOLE 3 AT OAKMONT

Known for its "Church Pews"—a 2-acre bunker sectioned by eight grass-covered ridges that are 3 feet tall and 75 feet wide—this hellacious par-4 is as tough on errant ball strikers as the steel mills of nearby Pittsburgh were on iron ore.

Continued . . .

4 HOLE 17 AT SAWGRASS

Although a short 137 yards, this par-3 at the Tournament Players Club in northeast Florida is considered the most emotionally testing single shot in golf, requiring pinpoint accuracy from the tee to a "postage stamp" island green. Over the years, it's brought the game's best to their knees.

WHEN IN DOUBT, BRING UP . . .

BOBBY JONES

Cofounder of Augusta National and the Masters tournament, Jones was the greatest player of the amateur (pre-WWII) era, winning thirteen major championships.

SAMPLE CHATTER:
"No one had a sweeter swing than ol' Bobby Jones."

A FEW FEARLESS FORECASTS TO MAKE

DEFINITELY!

Tiger Woods will win another Masters because, physical troubles or not, he knows the course better than anybody, and if Jack Nicklaus could do it at forty-six (in 1986), this gym rat can too.

POSSIBLY . . .

Someone will shoot a 57 over 18 holes in a PGA tournament, setting a new "unbreakable" mark, for video and real golfers alike.

WHY NOT?

Caddies will be replaced by robots, who will be a lot more efficient but significantly less colorful than current loopers.

ONE DEBATE YOU CAN WIN

Is golf really a sport?

THE PREMISE

Golf is a leisurely game of no contact and little physical exertion that is played against no defenders. The players, who come in all shapes and sizes, don't even have to carry their own clubs!

YOUR POSITION

Of course it is.

YOUR ARGUMENT

If your average score is 73, you'll be the player everyone wants in their weekend foursome. If you average 72, you can attend college for free. Average 71 and you can make a living; 70 and you'll be a millionaire many times over; 69 and you'll be one of the most famous athletes in the world. With a margin for error that small, yes, golf is a sport. Besides, almost every other pro athlete on the planet plays golf—and not one of them is good enough to compete with the best in the world.

RUST THE PASSER

RUSH THE PASSER

DeMARCUS WARE
NFL Linebacker

Your start when the ball is hiked is the most important thing. All good pass rushers have a first step that gets them to the offensive lineman fast so they can go into attack mode. You need to do something that gets the offensive lineman off balance, because once you do, you can control leverage. Like the swim move (see opposite), which can be effective if you're quick enough with it. It's a jab step–hand jab combination. The step is a quick one in the direction you don't plan to go—say, your right foot stepping a little to the left. The blocker needs to believe you're going left. That gets him leaning that way. At the same time, you jab the lineman's shoulder on that side with your right hand, to push him farther in that direction. As you do that you also bring your left arm forward, over and past that shoulder. Like a swimming stroke, except not as full. The goal is to get your left shoulder past his left shoulder, quickly, so you have a free lane to the quarterback. But the key is that first step.

Whatever move you end up using, you need to have a plan. A common mistake guys make is they don't know what they want to do. They just line up and say, "Okay, I'm going to pass rush." But if you don't have a plan, how can you have a destination? Every play is a chess match.

1

2

3

4

WAGER ON TEAM SPORTS

Before you go betting the farm on that sure thing you were tipped to, you should have at least a passing acquaintance with the basics.

FAVORITE/UNDERDOG. Pretty much every sporting contest features one team that is expected to win (the favorite) and one that's expected not to (the underdog). Bookmakers translate these expectations into odds that impact winning payouts. Place a bet on a 5–1 favorite and a $100 wager will return $120 if that team wins (minus a small commission, or "vig" if you're gambling at a casino). Back the underdog in a matchup that turns into an upset, though, and $100 will return $500 (again, minus the vig). Obviously, the higher the odds, the less likely it is that the underdog will make you rich. Know, for example, that even that 5–1 underdog is quite the long shot in the world of team sports.

POINT SPREAD. Common to basketball and football, spreads can be thought of as "balancing agents"; that is, devices to create even-money (no odds) bets that ensure equal action on both teams by using a point differential as proxy for the skill-level disparity between opponents. (If more than half of the bettors pick one side, oddsmakers will adjust the point spread up or down to attract gamblers to the other.) Say the Cowboys are 6-point favorites over the Giants. Betting on Dallas means you believe they will win by at least 7. If they do, you double your money. If the Giants win—or if they lose by 6 or fewer points and "cover" the spread—those who backed *them* cash in.

MONEYLINE. A bet in which the balancing agent is not a point spread but rather the cash risked. Thus, a favored team listed as −375 requires that you bet $375 to win $100. Meanwhile, the underdog in that same game might be listed as +275, meaning your Ben Franklin could earn $275 in return. The moneyline is commonly used in low-scoring sports like baseball and hockey that leave less wiggle room for point-spread adjustments.

OVER/UNDER. Another even-money bet, on the point total amassed by both teams. In an NBA game, for instance, the over/under might be set at 190. If you expect more of a shoot-out (with a final score of, say, 110–103) then you would take the over.

PARLAY. A combination of two or more bets, all of which must come through to pay off, at odds that are greater than the sum of the constituent bets. Parlays are a decent way to win big on relatively small sums. Then again, most of us have a hard enough time picking one game correctly, so having to do it multiple times is no mean feat. A tie negates that particular game, downgrading, say, a three-team parlay into a two-team parlay, and the resultant payout as well.

PROPOSITION. What are more casually known as "prop" bets offer action on any number of possible scenarios, serious and less so, beyond the game's outcome. For example: Will the first score be a touchdown? Or, Will the singer of the national anthem take longer than three minutes? Prop bets reach peak popularity around major events like the Super Bowl and the Masters, the better to entice occasional gamblers who are more interested in novelty than hard-core analysis.

GET LUCKY

Not every athlete in these sports believes in omens and talismans, but some of them do. And that should be good enough for any fans who haven't washed their socks since the last time their favorite team lost.

BASEBALL

☑ **GOOD:** Stick a wad of gum on your hat brim.

☒ **BAD:** Step on the baselines when taking or leaving the field.

BASKETBALL

☑ **GOOD:** Be the last person to make a shot during warm-ups.

☒ **BAD:** Forget to bounce the ball a time or two before shooting a free throw.

FOOTBALL

☑ **GOOD:** Wear double numbers (e.g., 88, 55, 22 . . .) on your uniform.

☒ **BAD:** Switch numbers after being traded.

FISHING

☑ **GOOD:** Throw back the first catch of the day.

☒ **BAD:** Change rods during a session.

GOLF

☑ **GOOD:** Start the round with an odd-numbered club.

☒ **BAD:** Use a ball with a number higher than 4.

HOCKEY

☑ **GOOD:** Tap your goalie's pads with your stick before the game.

☒ **BAD:** Lay one hockey stick across another.

HORSE RACING

☑ **GOOD:** Hang a horseshoe open-end up.

☒ **BAD:** Put a broom in a shipping van with horses.

NASCAR

☑ **GOOD:** Find a heads-up coin before the race.

☒ **BAD:** Eat peanuts in their shell before the race.

RODEO

☑ **GOOD:** Shave before competing.

☒ **BAD:** Wear yellow.

Continued . . .

SOCCER

✓ **GOOD:** Kiss a shaved head before the game.

✗ **BAD:** Take shots on goal in warm-ups (if you want to score during the game).

SURFING

✓ **GOOD:** Make sure one member in your group is too drunk to hit the waves the next morning.

✗ **BAD:** Announce that the next wave is your last of the day.

TENNIS

✓ **GOOD:** Walk around the outside of the court to switch sides.

✗ **BAD:** Hold more than two balls at once when serving.

ON THE TENNIS COURT

Because "that guy" loses playing partners quicker than you can chase down a lob.

DO	DON'T
Bring two cans of balls.	Bogart the always satisfying task of popping the vacuum seal of a new can.
Tap your racket in frustration.	Throw your racket in anger.
Rule close line calls in your pal's favor.	Call foot faults.
Accept the first three line calls made against you with good humor.	Ignore the fourth questionable call. Instead, walk to the net, look toward the spot where the ball hit, then walk back to the baseline—without saying a word.
Curse lightly—at yourself—if you want.	Grunt loudly.
Say "Good game" or "Strong effort" if you win. (And if you lose, for that matter.)	Say "Better luck next time" if you win. (And, for the love of Laver, don't leap over the net to instigate the post-match handshake.)
Compliment strong play.	Offer advice (unless asked).
Volunteer to buy a round after you finish.	Ask someone to buy a round after you finish.

CALL A GAME

KENNY ALBERT
Play-by-Play Announcer

First, get as much practice as possible. There are so many opportunities to do that today. High schools and colleges broadcast games—on the radio, on TV, even over the Internet. You can also practice into your smartphone while you're watching on TV or in the stands. When I was younger, I listened to other announcers and made a list of their key phrases. You don't want to steal exact wording, but you can easily learn hundreds of phrases and incorporate them into your style.

At any level, game preparation is very important. You have to learn as much as you can about both teams. Of course, you have to study rosters so you can automatically identify any player on the field. But preparation is much more than that. Games have lots of downtime and you have to fill it all. Baseball is the most challenging that way; on average, the ball is in play for only eight to twelve minutes and you might be on air for three hours. Plus, there are always surprises—a disputed call in football, fans throwing things on the ice in hockey. You need things to say throughout all of it.

There's a big difference between calling a game on TV and calling one on the radio. Obviously, television viewers can see most of what you're talking about. For radio you have to be more descriptive—about where the ball or puck is at all times or where the players are. If it's football, are they on the left or right hash mark? In basketball, are they at the foul line or at the three-point line? Far boards or near boards in hockey? Those locating phrases are key. But so is flow. You want to drop in tidbits about the players or teams in a way that doesn't interfere with the live call. Similarly, you have to develop a rhythm with your color analyst. In hockey, there's not much time for an analyst to talk during play, so when there's a lull in the action, I pause. If my partner jumps in, great. If not, I continue. In TV, there's a producer and a director in your ear, telling you if a replay or graphic is coming up or if you're going to commercial. That can be hard, but you learn to listen and talk at the same time. Sooner or later, though, you're going to respond to the voice in your ear on the air. It's okay. Everybody does it.

CATCH A FOOTBALL

LARRY FITZGERALD
NFL Wide Receiver

Catching a football is dependent on two body parts. First, of course, are the hands: you need to get them in the proper position as dictated by the catching situation. If you're running vertically toward the end zone with the ball coming from behind over your head or shoulder—a deep ball—your pinkies should touch (a) as you reach for the ball, ideally grabbing the fat part of it. If you're fronting the ball—it's coming at you above your waist—you need to square your body to it, while keeping your hands away from your body so the ball doesn't bounce off your chest. Create a diamond by touching the thumb and index fingers of each hand (b). That diamond is the bull's-eye for the point of the ball. If the ball is thrown below your waist, it's back to touching pinkies (c); they should almost form a basket.

But hands are just the half of it. You also catch with your eyes. That is, you have to look the ball all the way into the catch. Watch a replay of guys dropping a ball and most of the time they're not looking it into their hands. Instead, they're either already hunting for a place to run or trying to avoid a hit. So watch the point of the ball as it's coming at you, grab the fat part with both hands, *then* do what you need to do.

MAKE A MINT JULEP

You're not really immersed in the Kentucky Derby experience if you're not nursing one of these refreshers as the horses race by (in person or on the flat-screen). Our recipe of choice comes from Jacquelyn Zykan, master bourbon specialist for Old Forester Bourbon in Louisville, just a stone's throw from Churchill Downs Racetrack.

- 2 ounces bourbon
- 0.75 ounce simple syrup[1]
- 8 to 10 mint leaves
- 3 mint sprigs,[2] for garnish

In a mixing glass, combine the bourbon, syrup, and mint leaves. Using a muddler,[3] lightly press the leaves. Strain the mixture into a julep cup packed with ice.[4] Garnish with mint sprigs. Drink[5] (ideally with a straw[6]).

---

1. Make your own: Mix a 1:1 ratio of sugar to water, heat until the sugar dissolves, and let cool.

2. Use fresh mint. And slap it on the back of your hand to open up the pockets of oil.

3. A flat-surfaced muddler is best. Muddlers with teeth on the base will torture the mint, yielding bitter flavors.

4. Crushed, please. Juleps need dilution, and that will come faster with smaller pieces.

5. A silver julep cup is designed to keep the drink cold. Hold it at the top and bottom rims (not around the center) to keep your hand from warming the drink.

6. Once the drink has been prepared, insert a straw as close as possible to the garnish sprigs, so that every sip is complemented by a burst of mint.

BE CLUTCH

Three seconds left in the fourth quarter, at the foul line and down by one; bottom of the ninth, two outs, runner on third, tie game; 18th green on Sunday, one putt to win. Many sports moments beg for nerves of steel, a sharpening of focus and slowing of pulse that allow some to come through where others fall short. There are lots of theories about how to channel such Jordanesque stone-coldness; all of them boil down to the following.

DON'T STRESS THE STRESSING. The first step in dealing with nerves is to stop feeling bad about having them. Trust us, everyone does. Reminding yourself of that is surprisingly helpful.

TRAIN YOUR BRAIN. Guided meditation. Visualization. Mindful breathing. Whatever works is worth working on. Find your thing and use it. Nothing calms so much as knowing you know how to calm yourself.

THINK AHEAD. Spend some time breaking down what might keep you from being clutch. In particular, try to understand your stress triggers. Once you recognize that crowd noise makes you jumpy, for example, you can begin to figure out what to do to shut it out. In real time, having a plan is key.

GET IN THE ZONE—AND STAY THERE. It's a myth that clutch players are blank brained in pressure situations. In fact, their brains are filled to the brim with one thing: the task at hand. So, in the moment, focus on mechanics. Be a robot, devoid of emotion. Everything else—how you got there or why you got there or what happens after you leave—is beside the point. Sometimes the noise isn't coming from the crowd, it's coming from inside your head.

BREATHE THROUGH YOUR NOSE. Slowly. At least three times, right before you commit to an action. It just works.

WHO'S ON FIRST?

The only people represented in the Baseball Hall of Fame who never played, managed, owned, umpired, reported on, or were otherwise involved with the sport in any way are Bud Abbott and Lou Costello. The classic comedy duo are featured in Cooperstown because of their timeless "Who's On First?" routine. Can you name the players and their positions on Abbott and Costello's team?

Third Base: I Don't Know

Second Base: What

First Base: Who

Catcher: Tomorrow

Pitcher: Today

Shortstop: I Don't Give a Darn

Left Field: Why

Center Field: Because

Unnamed: Right Field

TAPE A HOCKEY STICK

There are many reasons to tape a hockey stick. On wooden sticks, tape protects the blade against breakage and water damage. On all other materials, it aids puck control by increasing friction. (Untaped blades are slick.) Does that mean you must tape your stick? No. But most of the pros do, and who are we to argue? Here's how to go about it.

1. Choose your color. Black tape can camouflage the black puck, making it harder for goalies to see it as it flies off the blade. White tape, conversely, makes the puck stand out, which assists stickhandling (the contrast makes it easier for the skater to see the puck peripherally as he looks ahead). Some other distinctive color will help teammates who may be looking down identify a friendly stick. So, if your scoring game is in close, go with black. If you're still working on puck control, opt for white. And if your teammates are head-down skaters, tell them to be careful!

2. Work from toe to heel. Yes, traditionalists tape the blade from heel to toe, which some say increases the spin of shots. But it can also make the puck "stick" to the blade a tad longer, reducing shot speed.

3. Choose your style. Similar to a unique color, a particular pattern—taping just the blade's sweet spot, say, or leaving spaces—can help distinguish you on the ice. Hall of Famer Bobby Orr, for instance, eschewed tape altogether, figuring his teammates would instantly recognize his naked stick in a sea of taped-up blades.

4. If you use a wooden stick, place a single strip of tape along the blade bottom, folding it up on both sides. This keeps out moisture. Then wrap the tape so each layer overlaps the previous one by about a quarter inch (see below).

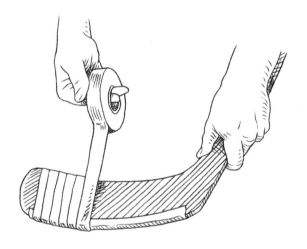

5. Flatten bubbles. Roll a puck along the taped blade to flatten bubbles and maximize adhesion.

6. Add a layer of stick wax or surfer's wax on top of the tape and along the blade bottom. It improves the longevity of the tape job and helps the blade glide more smoothly.

FRAME A PITCH

CHRIS IANNETTA
MLB Catcher

Framing demands constant adjustments, based on your pitcher's control and how the umpire is calling the strike zone. It sounds obvious, but the goal is to make the strikes look like strikes. That means different things at different levels. When you're in Little League (or even the low minors—anywhere pitchers struggle with control), you really can't do much more than give a good target with an open glove and be sure to catch the pitch when it comes in. As the pitchers get better, you want to treat the ball like an egg, cradling it in soft hands. Never jab; you don't want to reach through the baseball. That makes it look like the ball didn't go where it was supposed to, and you won't get the call from the ump if he sees that. You need to know your pitchers: Ask them to rank their pitches, what they might throw when, and what type of visual they like—a high or low target? Do they want you to set up on the corners? Some guys think of home plate as sliced into thirds. Knowing those things will help you call pitches that put the pitchers in the best position to succeed, but they will also help you get in the best position to make them look good.

The most common mistake a catcher makes is to work "above the baseball": He sets up for the pitch but unconsciously raises his glove a little higher, because it's a more naturally relaxed position. When the pitch comes in, though, he has to move his glove down, and that makes it look as if the ball is coming in lower than it was meant to. It's better to keep your glove at the bottom of the strike zone, then catch the ball on the way up if you need to. Even when you're going side to side to catch the ball, make sure your glove is moving toward the center of the plate. Set up farther outside, say, than you need to so you have to come back toward the middle to get the ball.

Some teams give their catchers daily ratings on pitch framing, both for their own catchers and their opponent's. One time when I played the Braves, who do that, their guy had like a plus one or plus two rating, and he considered it a pretty good day. He told me I had a plus nine. I must have been doing something right.

TALK ABOUT
YOUR FANTASY TEAM

DON'T.*

At least not to anyone who isn't in your league, and especially not to anyone who doesn't play fantasy sports. To paraphrase the old joke, the two most boring subjects in the world are someone else's golf score and your bad beat in fantasy.

IN A PICKUP BASKETBALL GAME

Because "that guy" might not get to touch the ball.

DO	DON'T
Ask an observer—or, better yet, a player during a break on the court—if the game is open.	Play in a game in which the skill level is obviously above (or below) yours.
Watch a few games, even if you lose your spot in the queue for "next."	Call "next" without knowing what the situation is like in front of you.
Pass early and often. (Nobody likes a gunner, especially if it's the new guy.)	Shoot more than once for every three times you handle the ball, even if you're hot.
Dive for balls and box out. Doing the grunt work elevates your cred.	Call fouls in the first few runs. You earn more respect with a calm "Easy there" than a quick verbal whistle. More likely than not a teammate familiar with the game's limits will step in soon enough on your behalf.
Be free (but not too free) with a "nice shot" or head nod for an opponent's good pass. Pickup games should be able to survive an across-the-aisle compliment or two.	Trash talk, even if others are. You don't know how some folks will react!
Keep an eye on your stuff.	Ask a stranger to keep an eye on your stuff.

COACH KIDS

Pretty much every youth league relies on parent volunteers. Yes, it's time-consuming, so many parents are unable to volunteer. But giving up some of your free time is a small price to pay for the chance to turn a ragtag bunch of uncoordinated kiddos into some semblance of a cohesive playing unit! Full disclosure: There is no magic formula for coaching success. But here are some useful tips.

GET AN EARLY START. Set your coaching career in motion when your kid debuts in organized sports, likely around age seven or eight. (Plenty of team leagues start earlier, but they are more for exposing toddlers to the rudiments of play, and, let's be honest, supervision in these leagues has more in common with cat herding than coaching.) Jumping in as soon as things get serious has its advantages. Kids often continue with a particular coach and group of teammates as they age. Coaches involved from the beginning get the jump on building a long-term dynasty unit and first dibs on promising players.

PLAY TO YOUR AUDIENCE. First-year Pop Warner players don't need to learn the Cover 2 and the littlest Little Leaguers don't need to know how to turn a double play. You may be well schooled in the intricacies of the game you're coaching, but it's better to show them how to block and tackle or throw and catch. Fundamentals first!

KEEP EVERYONE INVOLVED . . . It's a hard reality to impart some-times—or even to buy into—but the point of youth sports is not winning. Sure, you want your team to be competitive, but not at any cost. Sticking an eight-year-old on the end of the bench or out in right field to maximize your team's chances is only certain to result in a kid who doesn't like you and gets nothing out of the experience.

. . . BUT MANAGE EXPECTATIONS. All kids imagine themselves a star. If part of your job is helping them reach that goal, the rest is keeping them from growing frustrated when they inevitably play like less than one. That includes not setting them up to fail. If a player can't dribble without bouncing the ball off her foot, she shouldn't be your point guard. If a pitcher can't reach the plate, make someone else your opening-day starter. You're there to teach, not torture.

STAY POSITIVE. They may not be the star pitcher or starting point guard, but that doesn't mean they're not contributing. Find the thing a kid is good at, and play to that strength, reinforcing it with pep talks like "I really need your arm in the outfield" or "You help us most when you're grabbing rebounds." Affirming spin boosts confidence, and confidence boosts performance.

REMEMBER THAT YOU'RE THE ADULT. Your time on the planet has bestowed upon you something most youngsters have none of: the long view. It's your responsibility to keep the situation, play, bad call, obnoxious parent, or jerky opposing team in perspective. It's only a game, and how you react to it will make sure it stays just that.

DO AN OLLIE

Named for its originator, Alan "Ollie" Gelfand, this move is a rite of passage for anyone who wants to look like he knows what he's doing on a skateboard. Although simple in theory—you jump, your "deck" rises with you, you and your deck land together without wiping out—this Skate 101 trick takes hours of practice to master.

1. Put on a helmet. (Seriously, don't be a fool.)

2. Find a patch of grass. One day you'll Ollie on concrete as you speed along, but until then you're going to practice on grass—as much to keep your board from rolling as to cushion your falls.

3. Stand on your board with one foot at the tail (back) and the other near the middle. If you're right-handed, that probably means right foot back. But if you're not sure, set yourself up as if for a tug-of-war; that will show you which foot you prefer in front. It will also tell you how to stand on a skateboard in general: torso open to the side, head turned forward.

4. Position your back foot on the tail so you're on the ball of your sneaker.

5. Bend your knees into a squat.

6. As you jump, push down the tail of the board with the toe of your back foot, which will pop the board into the air (a). What should happen naturally then is your front knee will bend forward as the foot lifts toward your crotch (b). Your primary focus needs to be on making sure that your front foot maintains contact with the deck as it rises, sliding on its side up the board, as your knee rises and flexes (c–d). This should happen naturally, especially if you're relaxed. So relax!

7. On the way down, flatten your front foot and shift your upper body slightly forward as you level out.

8. Upon landing, bend your knees a bit. (Think shock absorption.) You almost assuredly won't nail the trick the first time, or even the tenth. But nail it you will, at which point . . .

CONGRATULATIONS!
YOU DID YOUR FIRST OLLIE.

9. Now do it again. And again. (And please don't rush to the skater park until you conquer it.)

BET WITH A FRIEND

Short answer: carefully. Because while there are many reasons to applaud legalized sports betting, the one least discussed is that it lowers to zero the chances that a friendship will be harmed after one side inevitably loses or, worse, loses and fails to pay up. You can't really get mad at an anonymous stranger on the other side of a sports "book" or app. If you must gamble with a pal, heed these four rules.

RULE #1: WE DON'T GET RICH OFF PEOPLE WE LOVE. A dollar's value is relative; what seems like a lot to one person may be pocket change to another. If losing a bet would hurt either side, the stakes are too high. That said, sometimes the point is to have it sting a little. In that case, make a bet that requires a service (loser mows winner's lawn for a month, for example) or eating crow (loser wears jersey of winner's favorite team to next public gathering).

RULE #2: WIN-WIN BEATS WIN-LOSE. Yes, bets feel most real when money changes hands. But money can't buy happiness. What it can buy, though, is a nice dinner or tickets to next season's opener—for both the winner and the loser. And thus a potentially friendship-fouling situation becomes a friendship-forging one.

RULE #3: SET CLEAR GROUND RULES. How much and, just as important, by when. At the risk of spoiling the informal nature of the transaction, we suggest a text or an e-mail to acknowledge the terms.

RULE #4: SETTLE UP PROMPTLY. Much of the fun of winning a friendly wager is lost when it requires chasing down the reward. Don't make them come after you.

PAINT YOUR FACE

DON'T.*

---

*Especially if college is in your rearview. (And keep away from your kids' faces too, unless they ask.) The one exception to this rule: if you're trying to get on TV (see page 98).

— 147 —

BEHAVE ON THE GOLF COURSE

Golf is the rare sport in which duffers can find themselves paired with others who are much better at the game. Such lesser players owe it to their more seasoned partners to follow the unwritten rules of course etiquette. (They owe it to themselves too; when one's game doesn't impress, one's decorum can.) Here's what you need to know before you slice your first tee shot.

ALWAYS

☑ **BE READY TO HIT.** No one wants to wait for someone who's checking his e-mail.

☑ **GIVE HONORS . . .** That is, offer the player with the lowest score on the previous hole the chance to tee off first.

☑ **. . . BUT VOLUNTEER TO HIT FIRST OFF THE TEE** if you're an especially weak driver and the longer hitters are waiting for the foursome just ahead to clear out. Not only does it speed up the game, it shows you're secure enough not to be defined by how far you can hit a ball.

☑ **KNOW WHEN IT'S YOUR TURN TO HIT.** Once on the fairway, the golfer "away"—farthest from the hole—hits first, unless she gives permission to a fellow player in front of her to go first.

☑ **WATCH YOUR FELLOW PLAYERS' SHOTS.** Remember, they're trying to keep their head down, so they're counting on you to track their ball.

☑ **PICK UP YOUR BALL** if you're having a lousy hole—on your way to triple bogey or worse—when playing with a better golfer.

☑ **PICK UP THE FLAGSTICK** if you're the first to putt out, so you can replace it quickly when the rest of your group is done.

☑ **COUNT YOUR STROKES AS YOU GO.** Historical accounting ("Let's see, my first shot went there, my second over there . . .") is maddening.

NEVER

☒ **INSIST ON GAMBLING.** It makes the game more fun for you, but not necessarily for everyone else.

☒ **STAND IN ANOTHER PLAYER'S LINE ON THE FAIRWAY**—that is, the route between the ball and the hole.

☒ **TALK WHILE OTHERS ARE ADDRESSING THEIR BALL** if you're within earshot, even if they're not quite ready to hit. This includes whispering, which is always louder than you think.

☒ **TAKE A MILLION PRACTICE SWINGS.** Two are plenty.

☒ **OFFER ADVICE** unless asked, especially to a golfer who is clearly better than you are.

☒ **WALK ACROSS THE PUTTING LINE OF ANOTHER GOLFER ON THE GREEN.** It may not actually affect the shot, but it can feel like it does—and golf is a game of feeling.

Continued . . .

☒ **LET THE FLAG WHIP IN THE WIND,** if you're holding it. That will distract fellow putters.

☒ **FORGET TO COUNT A "THAT'S GOOD" PUTT**—i.e., when a playing partner gives you the benefit of the doubt on a short putt after you've narrowly missed a longer one. Players have another name for this: cheating.

A GOLF TOURNAMENT AT THE COURSE

Conventional Wisdom: Attend the last day of the tournament, and "camp" at a challenging par-3 hole, or along the fairway of a reachable par-5, somewhere around where second shots will fall. Don't forget binoculars, sun protection, and one of those folding stools. It's a long day.

For Your Consideration: Stop by on "cut day," when the field of players is pared for the weekend rounds. It's a different kind of drama, but just as compelling, and there is less likely to be a spectator scrum. If you can, go the next day too, and follow a single golfer (ideally someone in the middle of the leaderboard) for the full round.

PLAY POOL IN A BAR

Inevitably, even the least felt-savvy among us find ourselves playing pool in some divey joint or over-screened sports bar. Either way, you don't want to look like it's your first time at the table. These rules will keep you safely out of trouble.

RULE #1: Don't gamble with strangers—and by that we mean never offer to play pool for money with someone you don't know, no matter how much worse at the game this person might first appear. And never—ever—*accept* an offer to bet on a game with such a person.

RULE #2: Reread Rule #1.

RULE #3: Even if you're playing a game that doesn't require calling your shots, end your turn if a ball goes in a pocket other than the one you had intended. The real players in the joint will know that casual head bob as you strut around the table is but a lame cover for the *Holy smokes!* in your head. Anyway, nothing evokes "pool cool" more than following a made shot with a self-deprecating headshake and a confident "You're up" to your opponent.

RULE #4: If you do find yourself gambling with people you know, play for a round of drinks instead of cash. That will keep things chummy.

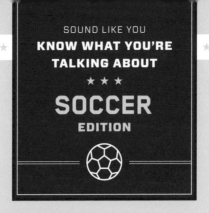

SOUND LIKE YOU
**KNOW WHAT YOU'RE
TALKING ABOUT**
★ ★ ★
SOCCER
EDITION

1 FIFA CORRUPTION

Soccer's international governing body has been beset by scandal—particularly involving bribes and kickbacks around the awarding of the World Cup to host countries. Despite a recent overhaul of leadership, reform will not be easy.

2 CLUB VS. COUNTRY

Soccer's league seasons overlap with important international tournaments, of which there are many. The grueling schedule has the best players weighing remuneration of club against pride of country, and much to the chagrin of their countrymen, the balance has begun to tilt toward self-interest.

3 WILL AMERICA EVER COMPETE?

The United States is among the world's best in every team sport it takes seriously. Every sport, that is, except soccer. Yes, it is the fastest-growing youth sport in the United States over the past thirty years. Yes, our top league—MLS—continues to improve. And yes, our women's team is the best in the world. But in the men's game, which is far more competitive, the United States is still, at best, a second-tier country.

WHAT TO SAY WHEN . . .

. . . THE U.S. MEN LOSE IN THE WORLD CUP AGAIN:
"Like I've always said, 'Soccer is a woman's game.'"

. . . SOMEONE COMPLAINS ABOUT LOW SCORING:
"You do realize that a 21-7 football game is really just 3-1, right?"

. . . A PLAYER MISSES A PENALTY SHOT:
"Next time aim for the guy standing in the goal."

MARQUEE TEAMS: PROS AND CONS

MANCHESTER UNITED

⭐ *Point of Pride:* The long-dominant force in the English Premier League boasts the most league titles (twenty).

❌ *Point of Contention:* They're kind of the Yankees of the rest of the world (see page 57).

BARCELONA

⭐ *Point of Pride:* Arguably the best in the world over the past decade, Barça, like their motto says, is more than just a club.

❌ *Point of Contention:* If few teams win more than Barcelona, few whine more either.

BRAZILIAN NATIONAL TEAM

⭐ *Point of Pride:* The five-time World Cup champions are famous for a fluid style of play known as the "Beautiful Game."

❌ *Point of Contention:* Beauty is in the eye of the World Cup holder, and Brazil has been that holder only twice since 1970.

Continued . . .

WHEN IN DOUBT, BRING UP . . .

PELÉ

This Brazilian striker of the 1960s and '70s was the best player the game has ever seen. He's Babe Ruth, but in a fully integrated way.

SAMPLE CHATTER:
"For me, nobody beats Pelé, and not just because he invented one-named celebrity."

ONE DEBATE YOU CAN WIN

Should soccer games be decided by penalty kick shoot-outs?

THE PREMISE

In tournament play, when a game is tied after ninety minutes of regulation and thirty minutes of overtime, the winner is decided by a best-of-five penalty kick shoot-out. Players from each team attempt to score from a spot 12 yards away, with the goalkeeper as the lone opposition. The one-on-one duel is weighted heavily in the kicker's favor, as basically three of every four shots are netted.

YOUR POSITION
No way, Pelé! (Sorry.)

YOUR ARGUMENT

A game should not be decided by a contest so lopsided that it is said that there is no pressure on the goalkeeper. (Hockey, which also breaks its ties with shoot-outs, has a conversion rate of well under 50 percent.) In fact, it has been shown that a kick placed just inside a goalpost is impossible for a keeper to react to in time to save from his starting point at the center of the goal. This makes the shoot-out more like archery than soccer. And while we have nothing against archery, it's been a long time since a nation's self-worth has depended on its successful execution. What's the solution? Some anti-shoot-out advocates suggest continuing sudden-death overtime play while taking one player from each team off the pitch every few minutes to open up the field and allow for more scoring opportunities. Sounds good to us.

A FEW FEARLESS FORECASTS TO MAKE

DEFINITELY!
International superstars Lionel Messi and Cristiano Ronaldo will join MLS. Together.

POSSIBLY . . .
MLS games will have higher domestic ratings than MLB games by 2025.

WHY NOT?
Globalization will come back into vogue, reducing the number of sovereign nations to one and making the World Cup obsolete.

Fun Fact to Impress Your Friends

Soccer players run an average of six miles per game. To match that distance, an NBA player would need to run back and forth on a court 350 times (which is almost twice as many times as they do). In other words, soccer players really are the world's best athletes.

FILL OUT A BASEBALL SCORECARD

Yes, it's old-school, and essentially redundant given that the same information is recorded in real time on countless websites. But keeping score of a baseball game is a lost art, and nothing keeps you as engaged. So plunk down $10 for a program as you enter the ballpark, grab your free pencil, and have at it. Who knows? You might be sitting in on a no-hitter, and you'll be the proud owner of a rare souvenir.

No matter what that self-appointed purist in the next seat says, feel free to use whatever symbols, pictographs, or hieroglyphics you want, so long as you can remember what they mean. The point is simply to record what happened to each batter on each play: how they moved around the bases, how the outs were made, and how the runs were scored. Still, there are a handful of mutually agreed upon symbols that make scoring universal. Each position, for example, is assigned a number:

1: Pitcher   **4**: Second base   **7**: Left field

2: Catcher   **5**: Third base   **8**: Center field

3: First base   **6**: Shortstop   **9**: Right field

Thus, a grounder to second that results in a putout at first would be scored 4–3, while a double play that goes from the second baseman to the shortstop to first base is scored 4–6–3. Other important symbols include the following:

K: Strikeout   **2B**: Double   **WP**: Wild pitch

ꓘ: Batter retired on a called third strike   **3B**: Triple   **E**: Error

     HR: Home run   **SB**: Stolen base

BB: Walk   **FC**: Fielder's choice   **SF**: Sacrifice fly

1B: Single   **PB**: Passed ball   **Sac**: Sacrifice bunt

Here's an example of how the following half-inning would be scored.

1. Lead-off batter walks = BB in lower right corner of box, with line drawn to 1B. Runner on first steals second base = line from first to second with "SB" written above.

2. Second batter bunts, advancing runner to third, but pitcher throws him out at first = put-out recorded as 1–3 across diamond and "Sac" written in lower right corner of box; draw line from second to third with "Sac" written above in first batter's box.

3. Third batter flies out to right, allowing runner to tag up and score = SF9 in box, and dot in lower right corner of box to indicate run batted in; draw line from third to home, and color in diamond to indicate run scored, in first batter's box.

4. Fourth batter hits ground ball to third base and is thrown out at first = put-out recorded as 5–3 across diamond.

TEAM: Drillers			HOME AWAY Asteroids			
UMPIRE: Truman			DATE: 7/1/1998			
#	PLAYER	POS	1	2	3	4
	Rockhound	4	SAC SB / SF BB			
	Frost	6	1-3 SAC			
	Stamper	5	SF9 •			
	Bear	3	5-3			
	Sharp	8				
	Andropov	9				

DRIVE 500 MILES

JIMMIE JOHNSON
Multiple NASCAR Cup Series Winner

It wasn't long ago that you just had to hope your car could go the distance without a mechanical failure or the engine giving up. Now the equipment is so great that the weakest link is the driver, so it's up to me to make sure *I* don't break down in the closing laps. The cockpit reaches 150 degrees and my body temperature stays above 100 for three hours plus, with my heart pumping at the same rate it does when I compete in triathlons—150 to 180 beats a minute. Studies have found that we lose the same amount of water NFL players lose on hot days—6 pounds or more. So I'm all about hydration, long before the race starts but also during, with a drinking system that feeds into my helmet. The hydration isn't just for the body; it's for the mind too. When young drivers go from running short sprint races to 500-mile marathons, their biggest hurdle is maintaining concentration. Those who can keep the same level of focus the whole time have an advantage.

Recovery time is also key. My weekday workouts are all about keeping my heart rate elevated between weight sets and keeping my mind constantly focused on what's next. I jump rope and run sprints, anything to teach my body to recover quickly. When you think about it, a 500-miler, with all its caution flags and pit stops, is really a lot like interval training. You go hard, then everything slows, then you go hard again. Strength is important too. Those weekday weight sets build the muscle groups I use in the car: wrists, arms, neck, back. During long races, those muscles are maxed out nonstop, not just from what I'm doing with them, but from constantly fighting G-force loads. I tell people to think what it would feel like to glue a 40-pound weight to one side of your helmet then go ride a roller coaster for a few hours. Then I say, "No, really, don't do that!" Because I do it all the time, and it's no fun. Unless you win. Then it's a helluva lot of fun.

A NASCAR RACE AT THE TRACK

Conventional Wisdom: As most speedways are vast venues that span hundreds of acres, altitude is your friend. Find a seat on the front stretch toward the top of the grandstand's lower bowl, preferably by turn 4. (Note: Don't arrive without ear protection—foam plugs or, better yet, industrial ear protectors. Seriously.)

For Your Consideration: Wind your way down to the front row for a few laps to feel that addicting *whomp-whomp* in your chest as 3,400-pound racecars hammer by at top speed. Also: Subscribe to FanVision, which lets you eavesdrop on each team's radio transmissions during the race. It's fascinating stuff, even if you don't always understand every word.

CATCH A BASS

JAMES HALL
Editor, Bassmaster *magazine*

Bass can live just about anywhere—rivers, streams, reservoirs, farm ponds—but that doesn't mean they are living where you want to fish. Before you do anything else, make sure there are bass there. Ask a local angler or tackle store worker if you're wasting your time.

Now think about what season it is. That affects where the bass are. In spring they head to very shallow water—as little as 6 inches—to spawn. As the water warms in summertime, they stay cool by going deep, up to 30 feet. When the water cools again in fall, the bass follow the baitfish back into shallower water, between 2 and 5 feet. But during the winter, it's too cold in the shallows, so you'll be fishing deeper again.

Next, you need to figure out what the bass are eating, because you have to imitate whatever that is. Walk the banks of the body of water. Do you see crawfish? Are there fish flipping on the surface? What are they? You can ask the local bait shop too. The lure is by far the most important piece of equipment; any rod and reel can catch a bass. You want to choose the lure color based on the water's clarity. If it's clear, then something subdued—a green or brown—is best because anything brighter won't look natural and will freak out the fish. In stained or murky water, you want something that can be seen from a greater distance, something a bit bright. And in dirty or muddy water, you need something that really stands out: black with a bright blue tail.

When you throw your cast, direct it toward what we call "cover"—a tree, a rock pile, a dock, or a structure at the water's edge—or to any significant contour change in the lake bottom, like ledges and bluff walls. Bass like hiding places from where they can ambush prey. Probably the most common angling mistake is reeling the line back in too fast. Slowing down, or even stopping, gets you more bites. An old man once told me: If you're being outfished, watch how slow the other guy is going and go slower. But don't get frustrated. Bass are fickle. Every time I get a bite, I'm still surprised that I was able to trick a fish as wary as a bass.

CHOOSE A TEAM TO SUPPORT

Most sports fans are born, not made. The teams you grow up with—the ones your parents or older siblings root for—generally are the teams you follow for the rest of your life. That said, for any number of reasons (relocation, say, or a recent curiosity about soccer), we are sometimes compelled to choose a new crew to call our own. It's a decision not to be taken lightly.

NEVER TAKE THE EASY WAY OUT. Nothing annoys lifelong fans more than a recent convert who chooses to root for the most successful or storied franchise in the sport, such as the NFL's Patriots (or Packers), MLB Yankees (or Cardinals), or European soccer's Real Madrid (or Bayern Munich). You know the guy who wakes up on third base and brags about hitting a triple? It's like that. Don't be like that.

AVOID HOT FLASHES. Recent success is almost as seductive as historic pasts, but be careful. You don't want to jump on a bandwagon of a sudden sensation only to find yourself explaining a season later why you had every team in the league to choose from and picked, say, the Bengals.

MAKE IT PERSONAL. You're an ardent supporter of scrappy underdogs (Pirates rule!). You're a citizen of the world (Spurs rock!). You really like teal (Go, Sharks!). Whatever your thing, pick a team that reflects it. The stronger the connection, the greater the joy when your team wins it all.

KNOW THE FACTS. There's nothing worse than a newbie sporting a Manchester City scarf, waxing on about one day seeing them play at Old Trafford. Manchester *United* plays at Old Trafford, mate. City plays at Etihad Stadium. You can't pass yourself off as a true fan if you haven't learned the basics.

LOVE CONQUERS ALL. If the only reason you've taken a sudden interest in the WNBA is that your sweetheart is a fan, there's absolutely no reason to root for a team other than the one he or she favors. Relationships are hard; don't make things any more complicated than they need to be.

> *Note: Unless you actually play for the club, work in the front office, or own a minority stake, you have no business referring to the team you support as "we." It doesn't matter how many jerseys you own (and by the way, you shouldn't; see page 253), how many games you've attended, or that you can name the 1957 opening-day roster. You win with them, you lose with them, but that doesn't make you one of them. There is no* us *in* team.

WIN A HOCKEY FIGHT

KELLY CHASE
Retired NHL "Tough Guy"

Hockey fights are not for the crowd's entertainment. When I fought somebody, it was because he had taken advantage of a teammate. Most of the time you're just trying to stop an opponent from taking cheap shots.

The key to winning a fight is making sure you grab hold of the guy in the right place. Wrap up his chest, and his whole arm is free. But if you get ahold of the crotch of his arm, down by the elbow, he has to punch through your fist to get to you. While you're holding him, keep your punching elbow up as you swing and turn your head away; don't worry, you can time your punches pretty well (see opposite). And be scrappy. I always liked to slip in a few extra punches whenever I could. If a guy was focused on getting his arm free, say, I might let it go, smack him, then grab hold of it again. The more you frustrate him, the more likely it is he'll give you an opening to hit him hard.

If I had a choice, I'd rather fight a big man. Small, compact guys fight fast, and with both hands. Big, tall ones punch more methodically, a fist at a time, so once I got in close with them, I knew I was going to do well. I never concerned myself with getting my target's helmet off, but if the opportunity presents itself, take it, because it can end the fight quicker.

I also preferred staying on my feet. I didn't like getting someone on the ground, because that's when you really get hurt. Most players aren't afraid of fighting; what they're afraid of is being embarrassed. That's why hockey fights go on until the linesman breaks them up. Unless a guy says, "I'm done." Then, out of respect, you back off.

RUN A FUN FANTASY LEAGUE

Notice the word "fun" above. There are many ways to keep a fantasy league afloat. Problem is, almost all of them are sure to annoy one or more of the members you've recruited to join. That said, some approaches are wiser than others. Here's a guide for staying (mostly) out of hot water.*

GATHER LIKE-MINDED PARTICIPANTS. Fantasy sports are meant to be a good time for everyone. But it's a good time for no one when, say, four hard-core owners are doing everything they can to win a championship while six others are clearly in it for the draft-night snacks.

DON'T BE A TYRANT. A smart commissioner runs his league like a democracy, proposing rules and parameters, then soliciting input from the other members. Will this kick off an endlessly exhausting e-mail chain that leaves some owners irked? Almost assuredly. Which is why you'll need to set a blind vote on the issue in question after a suitable period of discussion. Any crank who isn't happy with such a majority-rules approach is un-American.

ASSUME YOU'RE SURROUNDED BY KNUCKLEHEADS. It's on you to send e-mails far enough in advance to schedule a draft date and set necessary deadlines. Think ahead, because you can bet more than a few of your league mates won't.

COLLECT PAYMENTS BEFORE THE DRAFT. You pay to play; it's really that simple.

Note: For those rare times when things do get messy, see page 219.

MANAGE APPEARANCES. You know you're not cheating and we know you're not cheating, but nothing looks worse than when the random draft order generator puts the commissioner's name first. Think twice before you lock in your name at the top of the list.

BEWARE OF COLLUSION. For a commissioner, the toughest call is adjudicating one of those last-place-owner-deals-his-best-player-to-first-place-team-for-very-low-return situations. After all, there's a chance that last-place owner just doesn't know what he is doing (hence the whole last-place thing). Either create rules that prevent collusion (like a deadline date early enough in the season when most teams are still in the running) or establish a small group to approve trades. Whatever you decide to put in place, do it before the season starts—and tempers flare.

WIELD THE GAVEL WISELY. Not every transaction or gripe deserves a harshly worded group text. Intercede, scold, or harangue only when necessary. We're talking about a job with no perks; the respect of your peers is the best you can hope for. Earn it with evenhanded rationality.

NAME CHECK

THE QUESTION

Our games are rife with nicknames that became players' de facto real names. For starters, there have been five different "Dusty" Rhodeses (not to mention one "Dusty" Rhoads). Likewise, many jocks have legally changed handles for religious, political, or other reasons. Can you identify these famous players by their given names?

1. FERDINAND LEWIS ALCINDOR JR.
2. KEVIN FERGUSON
3. CASSIUS MARCELLUS CLAY JR.
4. EDSON ARANTES DO NASCIMENTO
5. JOSÉ GONZÁLEZ
6. RONALDO DE ASSIS MOREIRA
7. ELDRICK TONT WOODS

---

1. Kareem Abdul-Jabbar
2. Kimbo Slice
3. Muhammad Ali
4. Pelé
5. José Uribe
6. Ronaldinho
7. Tiger Woods

THE ANSWER

SING THE NATIONAL ANTHEM

Though "The Star Spangled Banner" is performed before virtually every sporting event—in leagues minor and major, at high schools and universities—the notion persists that those who sing it are elite members of a rarefied group. Put aside the A-listers we've watched at nationally televised events, and the average workaday anthem belter is someone—your friend; a neighbor; Mr. Nagel, the biology teacher—who auditioned and passed muster. Teenagers, Girl Scouts, and church choir representatives have all o-say-can-you-sung. And so can you, presuming you have the pipes. But please follow these three pieces of advice to lessen the chance of humiliation.

1. **LET THE TUNE SPEAK FOR ITSELF.** Patriotic Americans have been singing Francis Scott Key's number at sporting events since World War I, and it has survived just fine as is. As with any classic, listeners want to hear the version they know. Leave it to Beyoncé or Bruno Mars to embellish. You? Just follow the notes.

2. **LET THE PEOPLE JOIN IN.** The anthem was written in B-flat, a very difficult key to start in and still reach the high notes without cracking one's vocal cords. Don't make it so hard on yourself. Go with A-flat instead, starting on F. That's much easier for common folk.

3. **LET THE CHIPS FALL AS THEY MAY.** Once the song is finished, make a quick exit. No bowing or waving! You're not there for the accolades; you're there to honor a country and start a game. If you killed it, the crowd will let you know. (Good for you!) If you butchered it, they'll let you know that too—and in that case, it's better for all concerned if you're already on the move. (Better luck next time!)

ARGUE A CALL

Officials must be respected. Otherwise, it's anarchy! (And who wants that?) Then again, officials are human, and therefore at least theoretically responsive to polite persuasion. Here's a guide to effective disputation on fields of play.

PICK YOUR FIGHT. Periodically jawing with a referee, a linesman, or an umpire means you're into the game. Regularly doing so means you're a whiner. Whiners are ignored.

KNOW WHAT YOU'RE FIGHTING FOR. There's little chance an official will overturn a ruling. There's a much greater chance that planting a seed of doubt now will get you the benefit of that doubt later. The best arguers are strategic, thinking three fouls ahead.

FORGET THE PAST. Planting a seed, however, is different than bringing up a previous call. "You owe me for the last one" is a great way to get nowhere fast.

KNOW THE RULE BOOK. If you don't, you're certain to lose the argument. Worse, you're also likely to lose credibility.

ASK, DON'T TELL. Officials understand that heat-of-the-moment adrenaline flows will cause players, managers, and coaches to lose a bit of control. But they'll always be more responsive to questions about reasoning than accusations of incompetence.

KEEP YOUR DISTANCE. No one should need to be told that making contact with an official in any league at any time is the third rail of sports—the surest way to be ejected from the game and, quite possibly, suspended from future ones. Argue at arm's length; even coordinated athletes, when they're hot and bothered, risk accidental contact.

SHUT IT DOWN. Refrain from all side-of-the-mouth snark once play resumes. It erodes whatever goodwill your skillful seed planting has engendered.

WHERE TO WATCH . . .

A SOCCER MATCH AT THE STADIUM

Conventional Wisdom: Sitting midpitch, about halfway up the stands, offers the most comprehensive view of the action.

For Your Consideration: Infiltrate a section populated by one team's supporters to bask fully in the partisan vibe—the cheers, songs, and insanity. (Of course, depending on the home team, that could be everywhere.) Similarly, hunkering down in "enemy" territory can be a special kind of intense, say, with fans of a national team visiting a rival country.

SHUFFLE POKER CHIPS

Sure, it's irrelevant to one's card-playing skill. And yet, those who shuffle their chips at the table are invariably sized up as possessing an intimidating acumen at the game. Advantage: you. Here's how to fool them.

1. Grab six chips (three each of two different colors).

2. Lay a firm pillow on a tabletop. (A surface with a little more give makes it easier to manipulate the chips.)

3. Divide the chips into two even piles by color and set those piles side by side on the pillow in front of you.

4. Place the fingertips of your dominant hand on the pillow with your thumb and index finger on the outside of one stack, and your ring finger and pinky on the outside of the other.

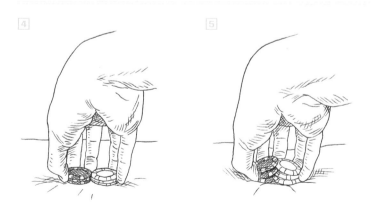

5. Gently squeeze the two stacks together with those four fingers, at the same time pushing up on the stacks with your middle finger, hooking its tip under them where they meet. Continue until the chips in each stack are at about a 45-degree angle from the table, and the two stacks are beginning to intermingle.

6. Push the stacks together to create a single stack, using your middle finger to guide the chips. If you have done it correctly, you will have one stack of alternating colors.

7. Lift the top three chips off the stack between your thumb and middle finger, then place that new stack next to the original, creating two stacks once again.

8. Shuffle again—and again, etc.—until you get it down, losing the pillow once you begin to find the touch.

BE A SPORTS AGENT

It's the dream of every sports-junkie kid who's not as talented as the best athlete in his high school: to represent that athlete when the kid turns pro. If only it were so simple. The players associations of the four major U.S. pro leagues stipulate that agents be certified before they may negotiate on a member's behalf. What follows is the basic gauntlet would-be agents must pass through.

YOU'LL NEED A DIPLOMA. The required level of education differs substantially from league to league. Only for some, though, is a postgraduate degree—MBA or JD—necessary, and exceptions may be granted based on negotiating experience. Still . . . stay in school!

YOU'LL PLAY BY THEIR RULES. Each sport provides what is often called a standard representation agreement, and agents have to agree to its terms. Sports may delineate classifications of agent too. The MLBPA, for example, certifies "general agents," who represent or advise players in contract negotiations; "expert agent advisors," who assist general agents; and "limited agents," who recruit clients and provide certain services on behalf of the general agent.

YOU'LL HAVE TO STUDY. Associations usually require agents to pass an exam that includes questions about the issues covered in the collective bargaining agreement—salary cap, player benefits, substance-abuse policies. (No cheating! There will be a proctor in the room.) Most likely, you'll also have to attend an initial certification seminar and return once a year to keep your credentials.

YOU'LL HAVE TO PAY. Application fees vary. The NBPA charges $100, for example, while the MLBPA asks $2,000. You'll shell out for annual fees too, but no more than a few thousand dollars (which will be a drop in the bucket once you start making the biggest bucks).

YOU'LL BE INVESTIGATED. That is to say, expect a background check. Red flags include having been disciplined as a member of a profession, dodging or falsifying answers involving the commission of a crime (not to mention the crime itself), suspension from college, and a past business bankruptcy.

DESIGN A SUREFIRE TOUCH FOOTBALL PLAY

The most important gridiron showdown of the year—besides the Super Bowl—is any game of touch football you happen to find yourself in. Considering how intensely the pros prepare for theirs, you owe it to yourself to come to yours with more than just a willingness to sprain an ankle. Like, for instance, one play that will turn the tide when the tide most needs turning!

THE GAME

You're playing six-on-six touch. The offense is made up of three receivers, two blockers, and a quarterback, who can't run past the line of scrimmage but can hand off the ball to any of the receivers. The defense has two rushers, who can't drop into pass coverage, and four defensive backs, who can do whatever they want but are most likely playing man-to-man against the receivers with one free safety patrolling the field. (Note: If your weekend games do not look like this, they should.)

THE SITUATION

This play works best when the defense has a fair amount of field to cover. So let's imagine the ball is somewhere outside the "red zone," with lots of running room to the end zone.

THE PLAY

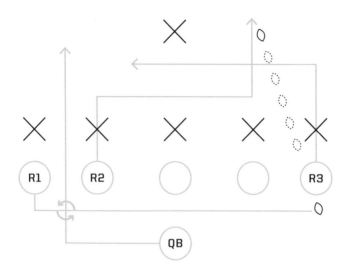

Receivers 1 and 2 line up wide left; Receiver 3 is wide right. After the snap, the QB takes one step to his right, then turns and scampers to his left as R1, who has feinted one step forward, turns around and runs toward the QB behind the line of scrimmage. Taking the ball, R1 continues running right, his defender almost assuredly in pursuit. Meanwhile, R3 runs a "shallow cross" (5 yards forward, then a sharp left turn) as the QB turns and runs downfield along the left sideline. At this point, the defense should be suitably confused, unsure if the play will unfold as a run or a pass. Then R1 stops on the right behind the line of scrimmage and sets to pass. In almost every casual game of football in America, the defense will assume a trick play involving a throw to the eligible QB. In fact, the safety is likely racing toward the QB's side of the field, a wise move given that R3's pattern has him progressing that way as well. (To make sure the safety does head in that direction, R1 should look left with purpose, pumping his arm to fake a throw there.) All the attention on that side of the field leaves R2 in one-on-one coverage. Better still, the combination of R1 heading right with the ball and R2's middle-of-the-field "wheel" or "chair" pattern (5 yards downfield, then across, before heading downfield again) keeps the latter's defender thinking short pass for a little longer than he should, allowing R2 to zip past him as he heads downfield to catch R1's throw with no one between him and the end zone.

THE RESULT

Touchdown! (Plus, years of retellings in which the weather worsens, the score tightens, and the heroic sound track swells.)

THROW FARTHER AND FASTER

VERN GAMBETTA
Former Conditioning Coach

Contrary to common belief, throwing velocity and distance are much more dependent on the body as a whole than the arm alone. The arm is simply the most visible segment of a kinetic sequence that transmits forces from one joint to another in a successive pattern that produces a single fluid motion. You *could* throw with just your arm, but it wouldn't deliver the power you need to throw at top speed or distance. The propulsion starts in the legs; further develops through the windup, cocking, and acceleration phases; then transfers to the core and upper extremities—shoulder, elbow, wrist—during deceleration and follow-through. What I'm getting at here is that to throw harder and farther, you need to increase lower-body strength, core rotation, and shoulder stability. And that means adding lunges, rotational core exercises, and pull-ups to your exercise routine.

THREE TOPICS UP FOR DISCUSSION

1 DECLINING INTEREST

Racetrack attendance is barely half of what it was forty years ago. Blame other accessible gambling opportunities, among other things. Heck, even the racetracks themselves now have casinos to attract visitors. But the big events—the Triple Crown and other major races—still draw. So maybe horse racing is just like many other industries: consolidating, not dying.

2 SYNTHETIC SPEED

Another sport, another performance-enhancing drug problem. Without a unified governing body or national regulations, this is a hard one to police. Further complicating the problem is the fact that some enhancing agents have important therapeutic qualities as well.

3 THE ROYAL THREE

Thoroughbred racing's Triple Crown—the Kentucky Derby, Preakness Stakes, and Belmont Stakes—is a trio of races of varying distance run over five weeks in the spring against top competition. Making the feat more difficult, some horses skip a race or two to be fresher in others. No wonder there have been only twelve Triple Crown winners in more than 140 years, and only one in the past 38. Which is why everyone goes a little nuts when it happens.

WHAT TO SAY WHEN . . .

. . . YOUR HORSE LOSES BY A NOSE:

"If he hadn't been carrying the added weight of my dreams, he would have won."

. . . YOUR HORSE LOSES BY A LOT MORE THAN A NOSE:

"Damn, I should have bet him to win the next race!"

. . . A FRIEND CASHES A TRIFECTA BET:

"You're buying."

THREE HUMANS THAT MATTER

1 EDDIE ARCARO

His five Kentucky Derby wins (in the middle of the twentieth century) may not make him the best jockey of all time, but his six Preakness and Belmont Stakes wins—not to mention two Triple Crowns—surely do.

2 JULIE KRONE

The first woman to win a Triple Crown race (the Belmont Stakes, in 1993) and a Breeders' Cup race (in 2003) and to be inducted into the Racing Hall of Fame, she stands as the best of her gender in this male-dominated profession.

3 ANDREW BEYER

This racing columnist created an invaluable eponymous rating system that takes into account a horse's time, the winning time of the race, and the racetrack conditions, allowing handicappers to put past performances in context. Kentucky Derby winners, we should mention, are very rarely horses who have not previously posted a 100 in Beyer's Speed Figures.

Continued . . .

WHEN IN DOUBT, BRING UP . . .

SECRETARIAT

The Triple Crown winner in 1973, his running times have yet to be broken.

SAMPLE CHATTER:
"If Babe Ruth and Usain Bolt had a baby with four legs, it would be Secretariat."

ONE DEBATE YOU CAN WIN

Are horses athletes?

THE PREMISE

They're animals, and as animals they don't really know what's going on. When they run, they're only doing what they're being told to do by their jockeys. They may as well be racecars.

YOUR POSITION
By any definition, yes.

YOUR ARGUMENT

Make this a purely linguistic discussion and there is no question: "Athlete" is defined as "one trained or skilled in exercises, sports, or games requiring physical strength, agility, or stamina." So no problem there. As for the eye test: Have you ever watched two horses—nostrils flaring, ears pinned—rushing neck and neck to the wire? If that's not competitive spirit, another cornerstone of athletic endeavor, what is? And then there's the opinion of experts: When ESPN listed the top athletes of the twentieth century, Secretariat was ranked 35.

DEFINITELY!

Riding crops will be banned as an implement of "motivation" on the racetrack, if for no other reason than to appease public distaste.

POSSIBLY . . .

Eventually, a horse named Horse will win a major stakes race—because all of the allowed names will have been taken. (See page 270 for how to name a horse.)

WHY NOT?

Animal rights activists and dwindling crowds will lead to the transformation of horse racing into a virtual sport, even at the racetracks.

Fun Fact to Impress Your Friends

The Kentucky Derby and the other Triple Crown races are open only to three-year-old horses because they were modeled after the English Derby, an older race contested in England for horses of that age. The word *derby* comes from the Earl of Derby, who won a coin toss for the right to name his race, beating a compatriot by the name of Bunbury. A good thing, because the Kentucky Bunbury really doesn't have the same ring to it.

GET UP ON A SURFBOARD

COURTNEY CONLOGUE
Champion Surfer

The method I use for popping up on my board is called the "Surf's Up Burpee." Even without a board, you can practice it at the beach (or in the gym) by drawing a line in the sand (or imagining it on the gym floor) and lying down on top of it. On a board, you want to grab the edges, or rails, at chest level, because that gives you more stability (a). But whatever you're practicing on, set up like you're doing a push-up, then use your core strength to pop to your feet as quickly as possible (b). As you do that, add a 90-degree turn so you land with your feet perpendicular to the stringer, the line that runs down the middle of the board (c). (That's why you practice with that line in the sand.) Be sure you pop up nearer the tail—the back—of the board than the nose. There's a reason they call it a *nose*dive! Your front foot should be no farther forward than the midpoint of the board. And your stance should be wide—as if you were riding a horse—and low, with your knees slightly bent in a squat position, for stability (d). Whatever you do, don't lean forward or backward or straighten up from that bent-knee stance. We have a term for what happens if you do: yard sale, because you're going to leave your board behind as you go flying.

WHEN ROOTING FOR YOUR TEAM IN PUBLIC

Because "that guy" spoils the moment for everyone within earshot.

DO	DON'T
Cheer/whoop/whistle when your team wins or makes a nice play. (Although a smile and a fist pump will also do the trick.)	Bang bars, tables, chairs, or other solid objects—particularly those in use—when your team loses or makes a bad play.
Remember that if you're in a bar, fans of the other team may be drunker, and crankier, than they appear.	Assume a stranger with a common rooting interest wants to be friends, especially if you've been drinking or that stranger is of another gender.
Empathize with strangers rooting for the other side about their team's tough history or current misfortunes.	Remind strangers rooting for the other side of past heartaches. They have not forgotten them.
Keep your deep knowledge of the game or its players to yourself unless prompted. No one likes a know-it-all.	Drone on pessimistically when things start to go south. Others may not appreciate this reverse-psychology style of dealing with adversity.
Offer relevant opinions about the weaknesses and reputations of players on the other team.	Offer irrelevant opinions about the race, ethnicity, gender, age, religion, or resident city of players on the other team.
Accept a high five from strangers.	Offer high fives to strangers—unless you've been bonding for a while—or hug someone you don't know.

BLOCK OUT THE CROWD

It's a challenge for every athlete: overcoming external distractions. Ask a dozen sports psychologists and you'll get thirteen strategies, but one formula cuts through the din: anticipation + preparation = immunization.

There's comfort in familiarity, and that applies to battling vocal and visual harassment at scale. So ask friends or teammates to wave their arms while you practice foul shots, or scream random nasty comments as you kick field goals or catch pop-ups. Focus has a muscle memory all its own; developing yours will make you better able to tune out taunts when it counts.

It also helps to take the time to develop a trick or two beforehand that you can apply in the moment. As with pressure in general (see page 134), a familiar routine, ritual, mantra, or visualization technique will center you in isolated situations amid a storm of equilibrium-impairing disturbance.

DESIGN A STADIUM

BILL JOHNSON
Design Principal, HOK

A stadium or an arena is a not-insignificant reason a team is competitive in the marketplace. When the building doesn't produce strong enough revenue, the franchise it houses may not have the money to sign the players it wants. So we're not just looking to build an interesting edifice. We need to create a destination. That is why our process always follows this particular blueprint.

PLAN AHEAD. Think beyond seats, luxury boxes, and signage—they can all be affected by economic cycles. Instead, we build flexibility into our buildings so they can be modified over time in response to a tenant's needs.

THINK OF FANS FIRST. You have to create a venue where it's exciting to watch a game or match. You want people to look forward to coming for the experience itself. One of our new buildings, the Mercedes-Benz Stadium in Atlanta, will reset the industry. Its retractable roof, which opens in eight segments, like a flower or camera lens, will be something people come to look at and say, "Wow."

THINK OF CONSUMERS SECOND. You have to accommodate people's expectations, including unhindered connection to social networks. New buildings must provide both the technology to connect and an experience worthy of sharing—"the Instagram moment."

BUT DON'T FORGET THE TEAM. Architects have to create a home-field advantage. Say you're on the visiting team and taking a shot in a basketball game, and it feels as if the crowd is bearing down on you and the basket— that's intimidating, if you're not used to it. Or imagine running toward the end zone or trying to kick an extra point and seeing a wall of fans screaming and waving at you. There's nothing like going to a big venue and experiencing that kind of crowd intensity. I look at buildings as stage sets, not only for the players but for the fans too. Design it right and everyone is an actor on the stage.

CARE FOR ATHLETIC FOOTWEAR

Commercials aside, shoes are rarely responsible for wins. Still, woe to athletes who don't respect their kicks. Whatever your game, check out the rules below; many apply to all athletic footwear.

CLEATS

☑ **DO:** Knock them together after games. Dirt and mud aren't just messy; they speed deterioration of materials.

☑ **DO:** Wear them in the shower. If you need to stretch them, that is. Then wipe them with a towel, stuff them with newspaper, and let them air-dry.

☒ **DON'T:** Scrape them. No sticks or tools. Instead, try a soft-bristled brush, which will take care of the gunk without damaging the shoe.

☒ **DON'T:** Keep them with the rest of your gear. No need to stink up everything.

RUNNING SHOES

☑ **DO:** Buy new ones every 300 miles (or six months). The interior foam breaks down over time—and when it goes, support goes with it.

☑ **DO:** Rotate pairs. Elite runners use half a dozen different pairs. You need at least two to extend the life of each. (Bonus: If you train in the same pair every day, your muscles will begin to get comfortable and, frankly, a little lazy. Rotating your shoes "confuses" your muscles, forcing them to stay in better shape.)

☒ DON'T: Use them for anything else. Not if you're serious, anyway. The mechanics of running are very different from those of walking, so the shoes you wear for each will break in differently. To ensure that your running shoes adapt to your particular gait, you need to let them rest between runs.

☒ DON'T: Throw them in the dryer. Washing stinky shoes is fine, but the dryer damages the glue most companies use. Stuff wet shoes with newspapers and air-dry.

ICE SKATES

☑ DO: Dry blades immediately after use. And when you get home, air-dry the boots completely.

☑ DO: Sharpen blades. Dull blades translate into skating discomfort. You should sharpen them after six hours of use on the ice, or just go by feel. For figure skaters, this will be when you start to slide upon landings. Hockey players can look for nicks in the blade. (Note: Figure skates require a specific sharpening method, and most rink machines won't cut it. Find someone who knows what she's doing.) But . . .

☒ DON'T: Sharpen blades too often. Like knives, you can hone them only so many times before they wear down.

☒ DON'T: Walk on the blades. It damages and dulls them, even on those soft rink-side mats.

WIN AT ARM WRESTLING

CRAIG "THE FURY" TULLIER
World Armwrestling League Champion

The key to pulling—that's what insiders call it—is positioning. Before you set your elbow on the table, put your arm—let's assume the right one—in the center of your chest, palm open and fingers facing the ceiling. Then touch your stomach to the table, and set your elbow down with your arm at a 45-degree angle. Your right foot should be forward, and you want everything tucked in tight, especially your right shoulder and lat muscle. That stays locked throughout, like it's all one piece. When your opponent comes to join hands, push your palm hard into his. You don't want even a small pocket of air because that makes you lose your hold. Once you set your palm, the grip is next. Push your thumb down into the meat of your opponent's hand, at the base of the thumb. Then close your hand so your fingers are flat on the back of his hand, your index finger pressing into the bone in the back of his hand that connects to the index finger. The worst mistake you can make is bunching up your fingers. When you do that, you lose grip and control. Now you're ready to begin (a). At the start, the idea is to pull to your left shoulder (b). If you do it correctly, you'll come over the top of your opponent's hand and turn his palm up, and when he gets in that position, he'll panic. Meanwhile, you use your weight to push down toward his elbow. He'll burn himself out trying to recover, while you're essentially in resting mode. It's really cool. One last thing: When you pull, don't turn your shoulders away from your hand. Twisting sideways is how you break an arm.

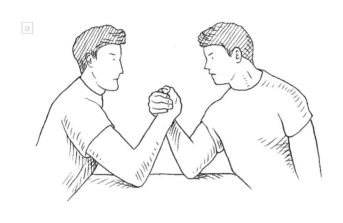

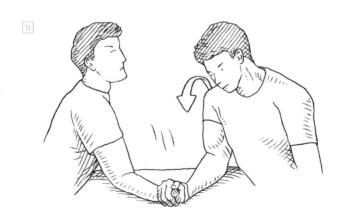

JUGGLE A SOCCER BALL

With your feet, obviously, because, you know, soccer! But this is no parlor trick. Any serious footballer will tell you that such off-pitch dexterity helps with on-pitch ball control. Here's how to put your best foot forward.

1. Grab a ball.

2. Go outdoors.

3. Hold the ball over your dominant kicking foot (usually the one on the same side as your throwing hand).

4. With ankle locked and foot angled up, drop the ball on your foot.

5. Kick the ball with your shoelaces (not your toes)—a short, quick kick, as if all you're trying to do is return the ball to your hands (because for now that *is* what you're trying to do; see right).

6. Catch the ball with your hands. (This presumes the ball has popped straight up to chest height. If it hasn't, keep at it until it does.)

7. Repeat steps 3–6 a few more times, until the move starts to feel natural.

8. Repeat steps 3–7 with your other foot.

9. Now, the tricky part. Repeat steps 3–5, but instead of moving on to step 6, let the ball drop to your other foot to kick. In other words: one kick with the dominant foot followed immediately by one kick with the non-dominant foot.

10. Catch the ball with your hands.

CONGRATULATIONS!
YOU HAVE JUGGLED A SOCCER BALL.

11. Repeat steps 9–10 a few more times, until the move starts to feel natural.

12. Repeat step 9 alone—twice—before repeating step 10.

CONGRATULATIONS!
NOW YOU'RE REALLY JUGGLING A SOCCER BALL.

13. Repeat step 12. Then repeat again. Forever. (Or at least until it gets dark.)

KEEP UP WITH YOUNGER PLAYERS

LUC ROBITAILLE
NHL Hall of Fame Forward

During the 1998 season, my twelfth in the NHL, I had hernia surgery. After the season ended, our coach said to me, "If you don't take care of yourself, your career is going to be over." That was a wake-up call. I began paying attention to nutrition. It's not like I ate a lot of junk food before then, but I made sure I got enough protein, the right vitamins, the right amount of water. I also recognized that what I did to stay in shape at twenty wasn't going to be enough in my thirties. Guys who last a long time are always in the gym, always doing extra. If they take time off, it's only to be fresher for the next game. You have to be in better shape than you were when you were younger. I also adjusted my workouts to changes in my body. When I began to feel a step slow, I trained as a sprinter. Doing the right workout for what I was weak at made me stronger on the ice. And I started to work out after the game, including icing down and getting treatments. I was more patient about my healing too. It takes longer when you get older; you have to be okay with that. In fact, staying competitive as you age has more to do with your brain than your body. You have to be a smarter player, but that's okay because you know more. You might not be as fast to the puck, but if you take the right route, you can still get there first. You can also figure out how to waste less energy. Ultimately, though, you can't dwell on the fact that you're older than most of the guys on the ice with you. Just play. In 2004, I led the Kings in points. I was thirty-eight.

WHEN TALKING TRASH

Because "that guy" finds himself on the outside looking in very quickly.

DO	DON'T
Needle strangers in an officiated game.	Needle strangers in a pickup game. You have no idea what their boundaries are—or how they react when those boundaries are crossed.
Be funny or creative.	Be scatological or crass.
Question an opponent's ability.	Question an opponent's gender or sexual orientation.
Get personal.	Get any more personal than you'd be okay with if you were the target.
Make promises to school them.	Make promises with your mouth that your body can't keep.
Double down when you're winning.	Forget the score. If they're ahead, keep your mouth shut.

OWN A TEAM

Don't have a few hundred million dollars to spare? Not to worry; you still have a couple of realistic options for entering the privileged ranks of franchise owners that don't involve marrying one. And that's not even counting buying into the NFL's Green Bay Packers, a community-owned, nonprofit team.*

OPTION 1

BECOME A MINORITY SHAREHOLDER OF A MAJOR LEAGUE TEAM

A number of professional teams in a variety of leagues are part of "public" companies; that is, their stock is bought and sold on various stock exchanges. In the United States, that includes the NBA's New York Knicks and the NHL's New York Rangers, both owned by Madison Square Garden Company (stock exchange: NYSE; ticker symbol: MSG); MLB's Atlanta Braves, owned by Liberty Media (NASDAQ: BATRA, Series A); and the NHL's Philadelphia Flyers, part of Comcast (NASDAQ: CMCSA). You'll find more options among European soccer teams, including England's Manchester United (New York Stock Exchange: MANU); Italy's Juventus (Borsa Italiana: JUVE), A.S. Roma (BI: ASR), and Lazio (BI: SSL); and Germany's Borussia Dortmund (Frankfurt Stock Exchange: BVB). You can even invest in Australian rugby via the Brisbane Broncos Limited (Australian Securities Exchange: BBL).

We didn't consider Packers ownership because the team has held only five stock sales since 1923, and it's not contemplating another. Pretty much the only way to acquire shares in the historic franchise is to inherit them or be adopted into a family that owns some.

OPTION 2

BUY A MINOR LEAGUE TEAM OUTRIGHT

Only $20 million or so will get you a Triple-A baseball team; even less—
$3 million—will wrest control of an Independent League club. And if you're
looking for a real bargain, you can snag a team in the very minor American
Basketball Association: the league will let you start a franchise for the low,
low price of $2,500. True, you'll need at least an extra few hundred thousand
a year to pay for salaries, arena rental, and travel, but there are currently
around a hundred franchises in operation, so clearly people are making it
work. And it's a diverse group of people at that; league officials claim that
75 percent of owners are African American, Hispanic, Asian American,
Native American, physically challenged, women, or some combination
thereof. And 10 percent are in their twenties.

NAME YOUR FANTASY TEAM

Hit the mark and, win or lose, you'll be the toast of your league. Miss the mark and not even an undefeated season will erase the memories of so many forced smiles and halfhearted chuckles. These dictates will keep you on target.

MAKE AN EFFORT. C'mon, this is important. No plagiarized names, pro or otherwise. There's a special place in hell for those who Google "best fantasy team names"—and a worse place for anyone caught doing it.

EMBRACE THE PUN. Avoidance-worthy in most other life situations, cheap wordplay says you're not taking your league too seriously—even when you are.

MAINSTREAM POP CULTURE NODS ONLY, PLEASE. Name-check bands or movies favored only by the cognoscenti and three things are guaranteed: (1) You'll quickly grow tired of having to explain your subtle genius; (2) you'll quickly grow tired of the eye rolls; (3) you'll quickly grow tired of being thought of as a self-regarding prig.

CNN IS NOT YOUR MUSE. References ripped from headlines will be rendered irrelevant by the playoffs.

USE GOOD JUDGMENT. We assume we don't need to waste time advising against anything demeaning, degrading, or otherwise deviant. But think twice too about that "clever" idea based on a disease, political issue, sexual position, or felony. It's not worth it; you can't be sure you know your league mates well enough to guarantee there will be no serious offense taken.

TROT OUT INSIDE JOKES. But only if everyone in the league is in on it. Otherwise, it's just obnoxious.

SLIP A PUNCH

YURI FOREMAN
Former Boxing Champion

The best way to avoid punches is to be the one throwing them! Otherwise it's about movement—of your feet, your body, and your head. Not too much, though. Overdo it and your head and limbs will be too spaced out, and that makes it harder to counterpunch. Let's say my opponent is throwing a right at me. My hands are up and close to my face, my feet are under me, maybe a little more than shoulder-width apart. But I'm not squared up; I want to be narrow. Setting my upper body at an angle offers less of a target—less real estate—to hit (a). Now, as that right hand comes at me, I move my upper body and head to my left—yes, toward the punch—a couple of inches or so (b). When beginners try to slip a punch, they turn away, but that's a big mistake. Here is how I think of it: Like any trouble you face outside the ring, looking straight at it gives you a better chance to deal with it. Besides, moving right just makes it easier for an opponent to meet you with a left.

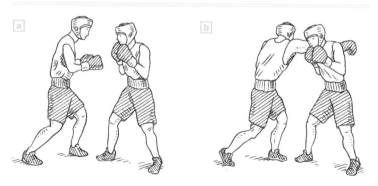

DISTRACT A FREE-THROW SHOOTER

Scream all you want at the player standing behind the ol' charity stripe. It won't have any effect after middle school. (And you shouldn't need to be told not to scream at middle schoolers.) Same goes for smacking those Thunderstix. By high school, most athletes should be able to block out such auditory distractions (see page 187). But there are other ways to get in the heads of focusing players. Here are three, starting with the easiest to execute.

1. SYNCHRONIZED MASS MOVEMENT

A bustle of random yellers and arm wavers slips quickly into easy-to-ignore static. But objects moving side to side *in unison* behind the basket? Suddenly, the shooter's brain is recalibrating to what it perceives as a moving background. It throws off the equation of the act. With a bit of organizing, you should be able to get everyone swaying to the same rhythm.

2. THE LONE HECKLER

A little tougher to pull off, for obvious reasons, but a sure winner if you do. Imagine the crowd whooping and waving and causing an ignorable ruckus as a player readies to shoot. Now imagine everyone in the gym abruptly falling silent and sitting down, save for a single person who remains standing to shout something—anything, really, although it should include the player's name—just as the shot is taken. Freaky, right? There's no ignoring that.

3. THE CURTAIN OF DISTRACTION

At Arizona State's home games, a segment of the student section behind the opposing team's basket raises a large frame with a pair of black curtains while a visiting foul shooter prepares his attempt. As he shoots, the curtains are pulled back to reveal . . . almost anything. Could be Olympic swimmer Michael Phelps in a Speedo and bow tie (in fact, this cameo caused an Oregon State player to miss, twice). Or a dancing Elvis impersonator. Or a large, mostly naked, belly-rubbing "baby." You get the idea. Only a Terminator could steel itself against such tomfoolery, which incidentally is not allowed in NBA arenas. In 2015, the *New York Times* found that the "Curtain of Distraction" usually gives the Sun Devils a one- to two-point advantage. So, yes, try this at home.

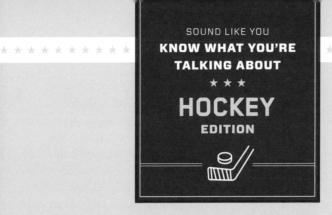

THREE TOPICS UP FOR DISCUSSION

1 VIDEO REVIEW

A rule added prior to the 2015–16 season allows coaches to challenge an opponent's goal by reviewing video to ensure that the team entered the offensive zone legally (i.e., after the puck). As with most instant replay iterations, this will inevitably cause as much controversy as it prevents.

2 CONCUSSIONS

As in football (and soccer and rugby and . . .), there is rising concern about brain trauma on the ice, which has led to rule changes that will hopefully make the game safer if, some argue, less physical. In other words, the way the Europeans play, and their guys are some of our best guys.

3 CLIMATE CHANGE

The NHL's 2014 Sustainability Report, the first of its kind, highlighted "major environmental challenges, such as climate change and freshwater scarcity" that will increasingly limit opportunities to learn the game where many of them do: outdoors. Plus, the carbon footprint of ice rinks in chilled buildings is not small.

WHAT TO SAY WHEN . . .

. . . HOCKEY IS REFERRED TO AS A BIG 4 SPORT:

"Did they stop playing college football?"

. . . YOUR TEAM IS LEADING BY ONE GOAL IN A PLAYOFF GAME LATE IN THE THIRD PERIOD:

"Am I the only person who wants to throw up?"

. . . A GOALTENDER LETS IN AN EASY SCORE:

"Someone tell him the game is more fun when you keep your eyes open!"

MARQUEE TEAMS: PROS AND CONS

DETROIT RED WINGS

⭐ *Point of Pride:* They've won eleven Stanley Cups, the most for an American franchise, which is why they call Detroit "Hockeytown, USA."

✖ *Point of Contention:* Fairly or not, the Wings are often criticized for depending too much on non–North American players.

CHICAGO BLACKHAWKS

⭐ *Point of Pride:* One of the sport's "Original Six" teams, they've been the most dominant team of the past decade, winning three Stanley Cups.

✖ *Point of Contention:* Basically, a reputation for cheap shots.

MONTREAL CANADIENS

⭐ *Point of Pride:* With twenty-four Stanley Cups, "Les Habitants" are the pride of Canada's game.

✖ *Point of Contention:* It's been more than two decades since this club (or any club) from hockey's birthplace hoisted the Stanley Cup.

Continued . . .

ONE CANADIAN POLITICIAN WHO MATTERS

LORD STANLEY OF PRESTON

The governor-general of Canada in the late nineteenth century donated the chalice that would eventually become the most famous trophy in North American sports.

WHEN IN DOUBT, BRING UP . . .

GORDIE HOWE

Detroit's beloved Mr. Hockey was for a long time the league's all-time leading scorer, playing a record twenty-six seasons in the NHL, the last one when he was in his early fifties. Yes, you read that correctly.

SAMPLE CHATTER:
"Gordie Howe was Wayne Gretzky if Wayne Gretzky could fight."

Fun Fact to Impress Your Friends

The tradition of the "playoff beard" was born of necessity. In the late 1970s, teams played on consecutive nights, often traveling from city to city to do so. As the New York Islanders made their run in 1980, several players didn't have time to shave before heading to the arena. They kept winning and they kept not shaving. Three (more) Cups later, a tradition was born.

★ ★

Are hockey fights necessary?

THE PREMISE

Fighting is integral to the game, traditionalists contend, allowing players to effectively police themselves and mete out punishment for dirty plays that refs inevitably miss.

YOUR POSITION

Not remotely.

YOUR ARGUMENT

If fighting is so important, why are there no fights in the playoffs? Also, why don't they fight in European hockey? Or, you know, in any other sport?

A FEW FEARLESS FORECASTS TO MAKE

DEFINITELY!

At least three young skaters over the next decade will be described as the "next Gretzky." (None will be.)

POSSIBLY . . .

Responding to complaints about low-scoring games, the NHL will widen its nets.

WHY NOT?

The next time the NHL adds a team, it will be in Canada.

BE A MASCOT

DAVID RAYMOND
Original Phillie Phanatic and owner of Raymond Entertainment Group

Ours is a competitive profession. If you're not adequately trained, you're probably not going to get one of the better jobs. There just aren't a lot, and the best and brightest and most creative performers get them. But there are steps we teach at my company to help people land a job and do it well. Above all, you need skills, particularly dancing, maybe even a little gymnastics. Mastering nonverbal communication is essential too, because you have to be able to show emotions and communicate ideas with just your body movements. So maybe take an acting class.

When you are confident in your skill set, find a job, any job—paid or otherwise—that puts you in a costume. Even if it's the guy who stands at the corner in a gorilla suit. At each job, capture some of your work on video for a highlight reel. And then start networking. Most performers get their jobs because they knew someone who had one. Some performers are very accessible; people call, e-mail, or connect with me on social media all the time. When you reach out, send your video and résumé, and don't be afraid to ask for a critique or advice on how you can improve.

Once you get a job, your priority is to get to know the character. Every mascot has a backstory: Whom does it love? Whom does it hate? What does it fear? Fill in that sketch with your own ideas for jokes, routines, and wardrobe additions. Practice everything you do first—in front of a mirror or friends—and continue to review performance tapes. And always concentrate on performing safely, so you don't hurt the fans, yourself, or the costume.

Speaking of fans: At the beginning of every game, focus on those who want to interact with you. Make a connection with one or two and the rest will follow. With time, you'll figure out how to handle every type of person, from aggressive adults to scared or bratty kids. For example, if someone screams at you, the best approach is to shame them: Drop your shoulders, dip your head, and act like you're crying because they were mean to you. But common sense is your protection. If people are calling you over for a picture, go. If they're argumentative or threatening, stay away.

DO A FLIP TURN

When most of us swim laps, we touch the end of the pool, then slow to a virtual stop as we turn to head the other way. How much cooler would it be to change directions seamlessly like Michael Phelps? A lot cooler, right? Here's how.

1. Before you get wet, find the "T"—the built-in cheat for timing flip turns on the floor of most pool lanes. The top of the T is where you'll start to somersault, leaving room to complete the maneuver without hurting anything.

2. Commence swimming. Proceed at your regular pace, keeping your eyes on the pool floor and your head in line with your spine. (Note: Every instinct will tell you to slow down as you approach the wall. Do not—repeat, *do not*—heed those instincts. You need to pick up speed. Otherwise, you'll lose momentum and be unable to complete the move— or you'll sink like a sad stone.)

3. When your shoulders are directly over the T, dive just under the surface as you continue to move forward, with your arms at your waist.

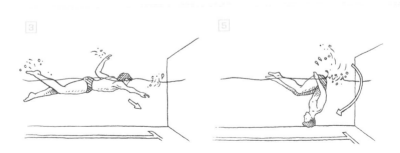

4. Immediately bring your knees to your chest.

5. Begin the somersault, using your head and core muscles to carry you through. Use your arms to stabilize and propel your body if need be, but return them to "streamline position" (pointing forward, in line with your ears, one hand on the other) by the time your feet hit the wall.

6. As you round off the flip—you'll be facing up—plant your feet against the wall with your knees bent and upper body parallel to the pool bottom. Push off the wall forcefully; kick!

7. Once off the wall, rotate your body belly-down.

CONGRATULATIONS!
YOU'VE EXECUTED A FLIP TURN.*

No, you don't look like Michael Phelps—not even close. Maybe you never will. But keep practicing and you will swim faster laps and impress that special someone watching poolside. (Hi, Mom!)

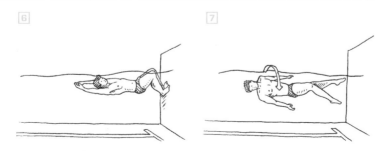

STAY FLEXIBLE AS YOU AGE

JORDAN D. METZL, MD
Author, The Athlete's Book of Home Remedies

It's pretty simple: The more active you are, the less mobility you lose. But what kind of activity matters. The biggest mistake people make is treating their bodies the same at fifty as they did at thirty. Mobility changes over the years, and your fitness program should too. To make your body maximally efficient as you get older, you need to focus on flexibility *and* strength. For the former, stretching is okay, but I'm a much bigger believer in foam rolling. Foam rollers—I recommend hollow ones—trigger myofascial release; they relieve tension by compressing the pressure points in the muscle tissue. I suggest rolling your full body weight for at least a minute per muscle group several times a week. Also, the effect of muscle strength on mobility is greatly underestimated. But that doesn't mean you should start lifting heavy weights as you approach middle age. Light weights at high reps do just fine.

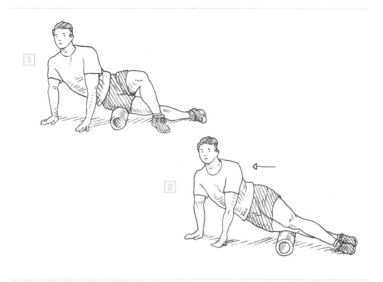

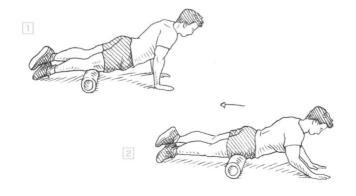

BE A BALL KID IN TENNIS

RICK MOZZILLO
Ball Kids Program Director, BNP Paribas Open

Most tournaments hold tryouts for boys and girls, ranging in age from twelve or thirteen to early twenties. I know of one tournament where the kids get paid, but they are normally volunteers. We give a generous meal allowance plus two guest tickets per session. Three hundred and fifty kids work our tournament, which is pretty typical. Most are players themselves, and that's great because you need to both understand the game and be fit.

Ball kids have to be able to work all positions on the court. One minute you're kneeling at the net, the next you're jumping up, running to the ball, then running back to your spot. You also need to be able to anticipate what will happen next—and what you're supposed to do and when, which is why knowing the game is critical. Our candidates take an online quiz, and they have to score at least 90 percent. If, for example, a kid doesn't know he can't return a ball while the point is being played, that's a problem. Ball kids cannot get in the way of the game. That's probably rule #1. Here are some others.

GO BACK TO YOUR POSITION after doing your job.

ASK FOR AUTOGRAPHS OR SELFIES ONLY WHEN YOU'RE DONE FOR THE DAY, but remember that if you're in uniform, you're representing the tournament, so be respectful.

TREAT THE OTHER BALL KIDS WITH RESPECT. And treat the rest of the staff respectfully too. Tennis may be an individual sport, but being a ball kid requires teamwork.

AVOID TALKING TO PLAYERS DURING MATCHES.

DON'T TAKE STUFF. If a player throws something—a racket or a towel— in the trash, leave it. Unless a player gives a souvenir to a specific ball kid, we want the fans to have it.

MAKE WEIGHT SAFELY

Athletes are obsessed with their weight. Bulking up, slimming down—they will do crazy things to get there. Wrestlers sit in a sauna in a rubber suit to drop the last few pounds before weigh-in. NFL linemen eat the whole left side of the menu to build immovable muscle. Mere mortals shouldn't try either tack, but we all can learn a thing or two from the nutritionists who help jocks do it the right way.

TO LOSE A FEW ...

ALWAYS

☑ **WATCH YOUR MOUTH.** A journal or photos of all you consume will keep you honest. Pay attention not only to the amount of food you're eating, but also to the kind (e.g., nutrient-rich or calorie-dense).

☑ **PICK YOUR SPOT.** Restricting eating activity to, say, your home (or kitchen table) means you will be less likely to buy a hot dog at the ballpark (or bring a bag of Cheetos into the bedroom). It's a psychological trick that is surprisingly effective, because it's easier to have a rule about process than to rely solely on willpower.

☑ **GO SLOW.** It takes about twenty minutes to feel full, even if we've eaten too much after fifteen. So drop your fork once in a while and chat instead of chew.

SOMETIMES

☑ **HIT THE SCALES.** Weight fluctuates constantly, depending on factors like water intake and "waste disposal." Who's to say which reading at what moment is right? And, anyway, nutritionists suggest a maximum weekly loss of two pounds, and incremental change like that won't register from day to day. One weigh-in a week is plenty.

☑ **MISS A MEAL.** Sure, you can fast every now and then—just not when you need to be on your game. Peak performance requires the energy boost eating provides.

NEVER

☒ **SKIP FLUID INTAKE.** Nothing sabotages the human body faster than dehydration.

☒ **GO TO EXTREMES.** What does that shrink-wrapped wrestler do after the match? Overeat, probably, guaranteeing that drastic measures will be needed again next time. That's one unhealthy cycle. Similarly, while excessively restrictive diets may work in the short term, they often have negative long-term consequences.

☒ **GET TOO EXCITED.** The biggest loss comes in the first few days, as you burn off water weight. Then the going gets tougher. Don't let the slowdown upend your long-term roll. Accelerating the plan will get you nowhere fast.

☒ **SKIP THE WORKOUT.** In fact, add an extra session, if you want. But don't overtrain. You'll put back the pounds quickly if you hurt yourself and can't work out at all.

Continued . . .

TO GAIN A FEW . . .

ALWAYS

☑ **DOUBLE UP.** Feel free to go back for seconds of proteins and nutrient-rich foods, such as most nuts, avocados, and lean meats. Still, go slow and steady: You don't want to add more than a pound a week.

☑ **PUMP IRON.** Eating lots of protein doesn't automatically translate into more muscle. You need to work out said muscles to help them grow.

SOMETIMES

☑ **AVOID SOME FOOD GROUPS.** Some athletes cut out starches and sugars entirely, which can lower body fat percentage. Problem is, certain carbs—bananas and sweet potatoes, for example—are also an important source of energy. Moderation is key.

☑ **GO MAD.** That's what the jocks say. What they mean is, drink a gallon of (whole) milk a day, for its hormones and high protein and fat content.

NEVER

☒ **TRUST A PILL.** Protein supplements sound like a good idea until you read the fine print: misusing them can lead to kidney failure, seizures, and heart problems. And those are the less scary side effects. Better to avoid supplements altogether. Oh, while we're on the subject: unprescribed steroids? No. Aside from the fact that you're almost sure to get caught, they're bound to do more harm than good.

SETTLE A FANTASY FIGHT

For all the myriad benefits humankind has derived from fantasy sports, we have not escaped without casualties: ignored loved ones, diminished team loyalty, and far-too-frequent usage of the phrase "snake draft." But no unintended consequence is more serious than the bruised feelings and broken friendships spawned by escalating conflicts over trades, scoring rulings, and the like. Many leagues avoid these sad outcomes by empowering their commissioner or a rules committee to settle disputes, but many others have been torn asunder when a neutral but known party has ruled in a way participants resent.

The ideal solution? Let the pros do it! For roughly $15 a pop, any one of several fantasy dispute resolution sites (e.g., FantasyDispute.com, FantasyJudgment.com, SportsJudge.com) will settle a matter quickly and objectively. Nonbelievers will say, "C'mon, who needs professional help to settle a fantasy argument?" To which believers will answer, "No one. Until they do." So set aside a percentage of your league's pot for "court costs." Whatever you don't use will help underwrite the season-ending beer-and-wings fiesta. If you do use all of it, you can at least gorge on the knowledge that everyone will still be talking to one another when next you gather.

INVEST IN SPORTS MEMORABILIA

DON'T.*

At least not unless the money doesn't matter at all. Yes, we've all heard the stories about the baseball card found in an attic that sold for half a million dollars, or a game-worn jersey of a legendary quarterback that went for fifty grand. They're the exception. There's not enough room on the Internet for all the stories about the saps who "invested" hard-earned cash in a hockey giant's stick or an Olympian's medal only to see the value of that piece of history halve within six months. By all means, buy LeBron James's used socks or Lionel Messi's shorts. But do it because you or someone you love is a real fan, with adequate display space in your den. Because that's where the piece is going to stay.

That said, if you must invest in memorabilia, please keep in mind that: (1) certificates of authenticity are as common as fake IDs in a college-town bar and even easier to whip up; (2) it's better to buy from a reputable auction house like Christie's, Heritage, Lelands, or Sotheby's; (3) before buying from smaller dealers, you can check them out with your state's consumer protection and attorney general's offices; (4) it may be possible to compare prices with other dealers or in collecting publications like Beckett, Tuff Stuff, *and* Sports Collectors Digest.

BREAK IN A BASEBALL CAP

In our style-obsessed culture, even basic fashion accessories make defining statements. This includes the baseball cap, a humble piece of headwear invented to keep the sun out of the eyes of nineteenth-century ballplayers that is these days a signifier of urban cool, sartorial chill, physical ease, athletic prowess, or tribal pride, depending on the wearer. But whether you favor a flat bill adorned by a "new hat" sticker or a worn and rounded brim spun around back, the cap itself should fit snug and secure. Sure, many lids now feature Velcro or button strips that adjust to individual craniums, but at the end of the day, these are but bootleg versions of the real thing. A traditional "fitted" cap is what you want, and these require the appropriate attention to sit just right.

Two methods work best. In the first, simply wear the hat through a few gym workouts; body heat and sweat will naturally soften the crown around your noggin. In the second, soak the inside of the crown in very hot water—that's right, fill up the hat for thirty minutes—then empty the water and wear the hat until it dries. As for the bill: If you prefer the curve, roll it and then tuck it inside a standard coffee mug, leaving it overnight. (Note: You can wet the bill first, sticking it in a container of water for a second, to make it a bit more moldable.)

TELL A SPORTS JOKE

Some people are funnier than others. That's just the plain truth. But everyone can tell a joke. Which is good, because everyone should have a joke to tell—to break the ice or break the tension, or to subtly redirect the conversation when it gets too esoteric or stat-heavy. Here's a good one to keep in your back pocket. And the accompanying annotations—by Jason and Randy Sklar, hosts of the sports comedy podcast *Sklarbro Country* and former hosts of ESPN's *Cheap Seats*—will help you kill with it, or any other sidesplitter you choose.

B **OB AND DOC**, lifelong friends since being the pitcher and catcher for the same baseball team[1] sixty years before, make a pact: The first of them to die must figure out a way to tell the still-living one if there is baseball in heaven.[2]

One day, Doc dies of a heart attack. Although saddened by his friend's death, Bob is excited[3] to learn the truth about the heavenly game. But he waits day after day, and still there is no word from the afterlife.

Just as Bob is about to give up hope, his cell phone vibrates.[4] He pulls it from his pocket and sees NUMBER UNKNOWN flashing on the screen.

Anxiously, he answers. On the other end, he hears a familiar voice: "Hey, Bob, it's me, Doc!"

Bob is shocked but recovers quickly. "Doc!" he screams. "You did it! You found a way to contact me."[5]

"You know I wouldn't let you down," Doc says. "How are you?"

Bob is beyond excited. "I'm fine," he says. "But enough small talk. I'm dying to know: Is there baseball in heaven?"[6]

"Well-I-I-I," Doc says slowly, "I've got some good news for you and I've got some bad news for you."[7]

"Good news first!" Bob hurriedly responds.[8]

"The good news," Doc says, "is that there *definitely* is baseball in heaven!"[9]

"That's great!" Bob says. "I'm so happy.[10] What could be the bad news?"

"The bad news," Doc says, "is that you're pitching on Thursday."[11]

---

1. *Note that the team for which they played isn't mentioned. This makes the joke universal. Had they played for, say, the Dodgers, the joke immediately becomes less interesting for anyone from, say, San Francisco—unless the story ends with the two of them leading unfulfilled, lonely lives.*

2. *The concept of baseball as being in some way divine is a well-trodden trope, elevating it above all other sports. Long before* Field of Dreams, *such idealization conjured images of Stan Musial digging in against Cy Young, Jackie Robinson stealing a base off Walter Johnson, or Yogi Berra keeping the peace between Ty Cobb and . . . every nonwhite player. Here, its "plausibility" serves as a classic misdirect, distracting the listener from the punch line.*

3. *Bob isn't the only one anticipating the call; so are we. A well-constructed joke engages the listener with some sort of mystery or proposition.*

4. *Bob keeps his cell phone on vibrate? So do many of us. It's the kind of detail, in other words, that paints Bob as a real person, not just a cliché cutout in service of a joke. Small touches like this draw in listeners while further distracting them from the fact that they're being played.*

5. *We're roughly halfway through the joke, and its absurd premise has been realized; Doc has connected from beyond the grave. Thus, the listener is dragged along. Actually, though, it is a premise only slightly more absurd than the fact that this eighty-something man has no trouble hearing a dead friend's voice on his cell.*

Continued . . .

6. *Note how quickly Bob shifts gears to probe for the answer to the burning question. It is this insensitivity to the wonderment of the moment that sets him up for an eventual knockdown. That, and his unironic use of the phrase "I'm dying to know" while talking to the deceased, has made Bob begin to sound like a jerk.*

7. *Bob is a jerk, but Doc is not. He has things to tell his friend, some of which may upset him; hence, the hesitation, represented by the drawn-out use of the classic setup. Instead of rushing through it—"I've got good news and bad news"—he takes his time. The best-told jokes slow down as they near their climax, to increase the listener's anticipation. It is no surprise that the best baseball jokes, in particular, move like molasses, as that is pretty much the speed of the sport itself.*

8. *Of course he does: Bob, as we now know, is an immediate-gratification kind of guy.*

9. *This is actually terrific news, not only for Bob, but for the rest of us fans too. And Doc knows it; note his excited emphasis. This revelation raises the stakes further for the listener—and sets up a steeper fall.*

10. *Bob's unnecessary declaration of joy here is essentially a verbal pause, subtly postponing the punch line.*

11. *Boom! The punch line lands, and like the best joke endings, it requires a two-step thought process that enhances the listener's ultimate satisfaction. The bad news—which initially might sound like pretty good news to an old ballplayer—must be unpacked. That is, it takes a cognitive beat to realize that in order to pitch in that heavenly game Bob has to die. And that, of course, is very bad news. The mental delay—however small—is an effective joke-telling device because it brings three distinct (albeit nonconscious) jolts: the accomplishment of having connected the dots, the surprise at having been "tricked," and the amusement at Bob's comeuppance. Because, let's face it, the guy totally deserves it.*

WIN AN EATING CONTEST

CRAZY LEGS CONTI
Competitive Eater

Some people are just born eaters. But for the rest of us, it's about adapting to the discipline of the sport. Like other sports, it starts with your body. How much can your stomach expand? How's your gag reflex? It might seem counterintuitive, but the ideal body type for a competitive eater is efficient and lean, without a lot of subcutaneous fat to get in the way of stomach expansion. And just like in traditional sports, physique takes you only so far—that's where conditioning and technique come in.

The trick to any contest is figuring out how to eat *that* particular food, as quickly as possible. A lot of it comes down to lubrication and liquid management. Take pizza, for example. At contests, you'll see eaters fold their pizza so the cheese is on the outside, acting as a natural lubricant to get the slice down more easily. If you're trying to win a sliders contest, you dunk the sliders in liquid to create a sopping meat-and-bread mess that goes down quickly.

Beyond physical conditioning and lubricant, professional eating comes down to mental stamina. The key is to figure out the amount you can safely swallow, and then do that for every bite for the length of the contest. It sounds straightforward, but in those last two minutes, maintaining that mental focus feels like pushing past the point of insanity. The best contests are those in which I'm so focused that the end feels like an out-of-body experience.

UNDERSTAND THE EMOTIONAL RANGE OF SPORTS FANS

The world of sports is nothing less than a prism through which the human condition is revealed—on the field, of course, but also outside the lines. And if you think that gives our range of games a little too much gravitas, please reserve final judgment until you witness the following emotions in action.

AGONY

Watch the first weekend of March Madness at the Caesars Palace sports "book" to witness grown men writhing on the floor as a team of much younger men knocks their bracket pick out of the tournament.

ECSTASY

Line the streets of a victory parade to bathe in life-affirming communal joy.

WORSHIP

Attend a Hall of Fame ceremony to meet dozens—if not hundreds—of people who felt compelled to travel a great distance to honor a person they've never even met.

HATRED

Sit in the visitors' section of a European soccer game to immerse yourself in a team rivalry that will likely make Alabama–Auburn or Michigan–Ohio State seem, you know, rational.

LOYALTY

Meet the plane of your team after they've lost the big game to understand the meaning of "through thick and thin."

REVERENCE

Stand in the gallery for the ceremonial opening tee shot of the Masters to support the legendary elders.

SENTIMENTALITY

Join West Virginia Mountaineers fans in a rendition of "Take Me Home, Country Roads" to see grown men and women cry for reasons that have nothing to do with the game's outcome.

TRADITION

Get to the Army–Navy football game early to watch a unique group of fans—cadets and midshipmen, respectively—stand on ceremony as they march in formation to their seats.

ASPIRATION

Splurge on a sports fantasy camp to see otherwise sane adults pretend to be something they know they can never be.

SUPERSTITION

Spend game day on the campus at Notre Dame to add a votive candle to the countless others at the Grotto near the stadium (even if you're rooting against them).

Continued . . .

AWE

Visit the racehorse paddock at Churchill Downs to hear even the brashest humans silenced by a wondrous athletic form.

OBSESSION

Mingle on race day in a NASCAR infield among the be-logoed fan base to measure how passion for a sport translates into consumerist loyalty.

NOSTALGIA

Attend one sports memorabilia show to appreciate how we never fall out of love with reminders of our youth.

COMMUNITY

Tailgate in the Grove at an Ole Miss game to experience how camaraderie—and a couple of six-packs—can overcome a generally mediocre football tradition.

NERDINESS

Attend the MIT Sloan Sports Analytics Conference to try to keep up as big data meets fandom, has a quick tryst, and gives birth to a thousand bouncing baby statheads.

LAY DOWN A BUNT

ELVIS ANDRUS
MLB Shortstop

You don't have to do too much. Basically, you just need to *let* the ball hit the bat instead of *trying* to hit the ball with the bat. We used to do this great drill in spring training: A coach fastened a glove to the bat barrel, then made us catch the ball with it. When you use the same motion without the glove, it usually results in a perfect bunt. So imagine you are catching the ball with the bat instead of hitting it.

Other things to keep in mind: Stay above the baseball—that is, focus on making contact with the top half of the ball (see below). Hit the bottom, and you pop it up. Hit the top, and it will be on the ground somewhere. Also, when I bunt to the third base side, I make sure to bunt before I run. Bunt first, then run—otherwise you may not get the contact you want. When I bunt to the first base side, though, it's different. I can run and bunt at the same time because I have everything in front of me. And sometimes I take a step in front of home plate, so even if I hit the ball straight down, it will be in fair territory. Other than that, I pretty much just let the ball hit the bat.

BECOME A REF

Whether they're patrolling grade school gymnasiums or Rupp Arena, referees and umpires are the unsung heroes of athletic competitions. And like all heroes, they didn't get there by chance. Here is how to set yourself down the bestriped path.

START AT THE BOTTOM. If you haven't officiated in Little League or Pop Warner or at your local rec center, what are you waiting for? Sure, over-invested parents, immature athletes, and self-serious weeknight ballers present particular game-control challenges, but anyone who can't handle the heat in these environments stands no chance in higher-level situations.

HIT THE BOOKS . . . Every league has an official rule book. Study it. Better yet, find a mentor with experience who can highlight the most valuable knowledge for you. At more than a few levels you will likely be subjected to a written exam, in addition to the "eye test" tryouts involving simulated or real-life game situations.

. . . BUT DON'T LOSE YOUR COMMON SENSE. Instant replay aside, officiating was, is, and always will be a subjective profession.

LEARN TO MULTITASK. Most armchair officials don't recognize how tough it is to sprint, maintain good viewing angles, and sift through a large number of irrelevant cues before landing on a correct rule interpretation—again and again—all in a taxing environment. How one juggles these various responsibilities determines future advancement.

HIT THE GYM. See earlier reference to sprinting. For all the jokes about NFL referees being middle-aged moonlighters, know this: those lawyers, teachers, and insurance agents are in some serious shape.

EXPECT IT TO COST YOU. There are fewer officials in the United States than there are athletes. That obvious fact bears mentioning because it means that as you rise through the ranks, competition for jobs stiffens. Those who want to work at elite levels need to spend time and money on continued training by professionals.

DON'T EXPECT IT TO PAY OFF. At least not in the beginning. High school basketball refs might make $100 a game, if they're lucky. College refs who work the marquee conferences in Division I may get $3,000 a game. Sure, veteran NBA referees can earn upward of half a million dollars a year, but 99 percent of officials never sniff that kind of comp.

THICKEN YOUR SKIN. Boo birds in the stands are annoying, but like serious athletes, high-level officials have to learn to tune them out as much as possible (see page 187). Social media criticism too. And then there's the intense postgame scrutiny of fellow crew members and league overseers. If you are one to respond defensively to critiques, this job is most definitely not for you.

PRACTICE PUBLIC SPEAKING. Depending on the sport, at the higher levels you may be expected to explain calls to packed stadiums. Start to get comfortable talking to thousands of half-drunk, mostly hostile strangers now.

THROW A RINGER

ALAN FRANCIS
Champion Horseshoe Pitcher

At the World Championships, where there are maybe nine hundred competitors, everyone basically pitches the same way: underhand motion, one step toward the stake, and then throw. That's it. But look closer and you'll see they are all throwing a bit differently. One person's downswing is quicker than another's. There are short backswings and long ones, short and long steps. Some throw the shoe high; others throw a low, hard, driving shoe. However you do it, the most important thing is to *repeat the routine every time.* Like with free throws in basketball, it has to be second nature. There are really only three places you should hold a shoe—on either side or in the middle—and where you hold it determines how it will turn in the air. Figuring out which spot works best for you is a matter of trial and error.

Start off by doing what comes naturally, which is usually how you grip a shoe the first time you pick it up. You want the shoe to be fully open when it gets to the stake, because that offers the most coverage to account for inaccuracy. The opening is only 3½ inches and the stake is 1 inch thick, so pitching from 40 feet doesn't leave much margin for error.

My own routine is pretty simple. I hold the shoe in my right hand, between my fingers, a little more than halfway down (see opposite). My eyes are focused on the target. That's important; don't ever take your eyes off the target. I bring my hand with the shoe up to my face and pause. Then I bring my arm down and back, smoothly, as I bend my right knee a little and take a big step with my left leg. Maintaining my balance throughout the pitch, I finish with my right leg slightly raised. The key is getting my body weight going forward; it creates momentum for the throw. My arm acts more like a pendulum; it doesn't do a lot of the work. That's what you need to understand. The arm holds and releases the shoe, obviously, but the body controls the pitch.

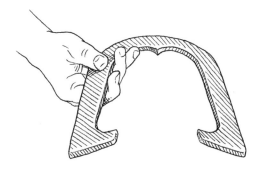

GET A JOB IN SPORTS

You may not have the chops to go pro, but your love of the game can still get you paid. Here's a selection of careers that will keep you action-adjacent well past the age athletes retire.

OCCUPATION	GOOD TO HAVE	GOOD TO KNOW	STARTING SALARY *
Analytics	Advanced degree in mathematics or economics; training in video editing and manipulation.	Sports industry employers increasingly prefer a data background. If you've never been to the annual MIT Sloan Sports Analytics Conference, buy a ticket for next year's gathering.	$57,490
Athletic Trainer	Bachelor's degree in athletic training, kinesiology, or physical therapy. So take anatomy, physiology, and physics courses in high school and college. And because it's never too early to head down the path, join the National Athletic Trainers' Association as a student.	The road to the pros: smaller colleges or minor leagues to bigger colleges to big leagues.	$31,640

Based on 25th percentile of pay range. Salaries fluctuate according to location, market size, and experience. Source: Bureau of Labor Statistics

OCCUPATION	GOOD TO HAVE	GOOD TO KNOW	STARTING SALARY
Equipment Managers/ Assistants	Bachelor's degree in business or physical education preferred. The Athletic Equipment Managers Association, of which you should become a member, offers college scholarships.	Maybe this is a thankless job, but you're literally as close as you can get to the action. And you can begin honing your skills in high school and college.	$25,000**
Marketing/ Promotions	Bachelor's degree in marketing or social media marketing.	Check out the informative blog and podcasts of the Warsaw Sports Marketing Center at the University of Oregon.	$44,950
Media/ Broadcasting	Bachelor's degree in journalism, multimedia, or broadcasting.	Different types of experience—in writing, production, podcasting, and video—will enhance your marketability. Media outlets increasingly want multitool players.	$26,640
Nutritionist	Bachelor's degree in nutritional science.	An internship at one of the "performance institutes" that players attend looks good on a résumé.	$33,870

**25th percentile figure not available; salary is average starting pay for assistants. Source: Bureau of Labor Statistics

Continued . . .

OCCUPATION	GOOD TO HAVE	GOOD TO KNOW	STARTING SALARY
Public Relations/ Media Relations	Bachelor's degree in public relations, journalism, communications, English, or business administration.	An internship with the sports information department at your college looks good on a résumé.	$41,520
Sales	High school diploma or equivalent; marketing degree preferred.	More than half the jobs posted on WorkInSports.com include the word *sales*. Think: tickets, corporate suites, ads, sponsorships.	$30,320
Stadium/Arena Operations	Bachelor's degree in facilities management or business administration.	You get to be in charge of all those concession stand sponsorship deals!	$57,360
Turf Management	Bachelor's degree or certificate in turf management or agronomy.	The perfect gig for 4H types who like to geek out on science and sports.	$20,420

OCCUPATION	GOOD TO HAVE	GOOD TO KNOW	STARTING SALARY
Umpiring/ Refereeing/ Officiating	High school diploma or equivalent.	Ask a local officials' association if you can sit in on meetings. It's an efficient way to learn the trade and get acquainted with the community. A first step in city prep leagues could lead to a jump to the college or minor league level and, maybe, even the pros (see page 230).	$20,230
Web Developer	Bachelor's degree in web development, computer science, programming, or information technology.	This rapidly growing field offers lots of opportunities in social media, content development, and e-sports. Good place to start: an internship at your college's athletic website or TV or radio station.	$46,600

BUY A SCALPED TICKET– WITHOUT OVERPAYING

StubHub has made the sold-out game virtually obsolete. If you're willing to pay, there will be a ticket for you. But if there are deals to be had on the resale market, they are much more likely to be made not online but on the ground with scalpers who lurk outside the stadium. Most of them know what they're doing, and aren't likely to be taken advantage of. But they are, in the end, salespeople who would rather not get stuck with unused inventory. Will there be games where scarcity will keep you on the outside looking in? Sure. Are there some localities where anti-scalping laws are periodically enforced? Yes. Should you be worried that the ticket you're buying is counterfeit? Definitely. But if you're willing to risk it . . .

BE PATIENT. The closer to kickoff (or tipoff or first pitch) you get, the more desperate sellers become. Once the national anthem plays, the transactional advantage officially swings to the buyer; just like that, you are negotiating from a position of strength.

DON'T BE AFRAID TO WALK AWAY. Anyone holding unwanted tickets needs you more than you need them. They're almost certain to chase you to offer a better price.

HIDE YOUR LOYALTY. If you're buying as a visiting fan, do not wear your team's colors—not until you've closed the deal, anyway. Rival fans rarely get discounts.

FLAUNT YOUR LOYALTY. On the other hand, some diehards with extra tickets may just want to make sure a like-minded compatriot will be occupying the seat. Those kinds of people usually get to games early. So should you.

TARGET NONPROFESSIONALS. Fans who seem like one-off sellers rather than daily entrepreneurs—their tentative "patter" usually gives them away—will not be particularly well versed about scalping economics. So your chances of getting a submarket price are much greater.

GO WHERE THE GROUPS ARE. Prowl the big tailgate parties and stalk the buses that transport fans. Chances are, someone in those groups didn't show up, leaving somebody else holding an extra ticket.

> *Note: Don't forget that you're literally making a deal with a random stranger, so if you're with a friend, offer to buy your tickets only after one has been successfully scanned at the turnstile and you are safely in. It's a long-shot ask, but some scalpers will honor the request.*

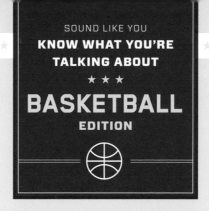

THREE TOPICS UP FOR DISCUSSION

1 SUPER PAYCHECKS

Why does it seem as if every NBA player is signing a gigantic contract? Credit new and very lucrative broadcast TV deals that caused the first of two big recalibrations in the league salary cap in 2016, giving teams all kinds of financial freedom to throw cash at the players.

2 NUMBERS RUNNING

Sports have always gone hand in hand with statistics. These days, those statistics—or metrics, to those who decode them—burrow deeper than ever before. And in no sport is this more the case than in basketball. But knowing who shoots best from where can get you only so far.

3 BOMBS AWAY

The three-point shot, which was almost a novelty when it was introduced to the NBA in 1979, has since become the centerpiece of many teams' offense. While most fans marvel at the skill required to score from such long distances—and relish the excitement these shots bring—diehards think a crucial part of the game is lost when so much of the action happens away from the basket.

WHAT TO SAY WHEN . . .

. . . SOMEONE SAYS THE GAME WAS BETTER BACK WHEN:

"You mean when players weren't allowed to dribble? Things change, Grandpa!"

. . . SOMEONE MENTIONS THE WNBA:

"The only pro league where players become less famous after college."

. . . SOMEONE BADMOUTHS COMMERCIAL LOGOS ON UNIFORMS:

"You do realize what that big ol' swoosh on their shoes stands for, right?"

MARQUEE TEAMS: PROS AND CONS

BOSTON CELTICS

⭐ *Point of Pride:* The most championship banners hanging from an NBA ceiling:

❌ *Point of Contention:* The rafters aren't getting any more crowded; the Celts have added only one championship in the past thirty years.

LOS ANGELES LAKERS

⭐ *Point of Pride:* Boston's principal rival for historic supremacy (one fewer championship) has the best courtside celebrity row.

❌ *Point of Contention:* The Lakers are no longer even the most competitive team in town. The Clippers have surpassed them as Hollywood's best team.

SAN ANTONIO SPURS

⭐ *Point of Pride:* Unceasing team-first excellence and Gregg Popovich, the best coach ever.

❌ *Point of Contention:* A style of play that's even more boring than it is effective.

Continued . . .

WHEN IN DOUBT, BRING UP . . .

JERRY WEST

The legendary Los Angeles Laker was one of the top-scoring guards of all time.

SAMPLE CHATTER:

"There's only one guy whose silhouette is the league logo—Jerry West."

ONE DEBATE YOU CAN WIN

Should kids have to go to college before playing in the NBA?

THE PREMISE

For forty years beginning in the 1970s, high school graduates were allowed to enter the NBA draft. But in recent years, players have had to spend one year in college (or in a pro league overseas) before making the leap, under the theory that success in the league is contingent on a bit more maturation.

YOUR POSITION
Absolutely not.

YOUR ARGUMENT

If somebody is willing to pay them for doing a job, why should anyone deny them? For the game's sake, however, most young players could use some seasoning before hitting the big time. The problem is, that seasoning may exist at the college level, but only if kids stay in school long enough to benefit. And why would they?

They're not getting paid and in too many cases are not getting much out of their classwork, if only because they're required to spend so much time on the court. None of us is as good as we could be in the first year of any job. Why should basketball players have to be?

DEFINITELY!
The NBA expands to London to capitalize on a growing international market.

POSSIBLY . . .
Rims are raised from 10 to 12 feet because the game has become too easy.

WHY NOT?
A four-point line will be added, because the game has become too predictable.

Fun Fact to Impress Your Friends

Why is the shot clock 24 seconds? What seems arbitrary is just simple math. Before the shot clock was implemented, teams protected their leads by holding the ball. Effective, yes, but dull. Syracuse Nationals owner Danny Biasone proposed a limit for each possession. He gathered a group of college athletes and pros and watched them play. When they were done, he divided the total number of shots into the game's total time and found an average of one attempt every 24 seconds. The rule was adopted in 1954—and scoring immediately jumped.

COUNT IN TOUCH FOOTBALL

One of the hallmarks of early-age backyard games—counting off the time before touch-football defenders may rush the quarterback—is also the flash point of too many advanced-age dustups. The key is keeping things simple. So . . .

IDEAL

"ONE | MIS | SIS | SIP | PI | TWO | MIS | SIS | SIP | PI | THREE | MIS | SIS | SIP | PI . . ."

. . . and so on, with each count expressed as a well-enunciated five syllables.

ACCEPTABLE

"ONE | ONE | THOU- | SAND | TWO | ONE | THOU- | SAND | THREE | ONE | THOU- | SAND . . ."

. . . and so on, with each count expressed as a well-enunciated four syllables.

Either should be said loudly by one defensive lineman at a reasonable cadence—because if the objective is not reasonableness, why count at all?—with rushing to commence only after the count is complete.

CLOSE A CUT

JACOB "STITCH" DURAN
Professional MMA and Boxing Cutman

I'm working long before anyone gets hit. While in the dressing room before the bout, I talk to fighters about medications they might be taking—particularly blood thinners and anti-inflammatories—and their medical histories, such as if they're susceptible to nosebleeds. I also want to know what kind of fight they envision, so I know what to prepare for. Mostly, though, I get ready for worst-case scenarios. I pack a Qwick-AID, which is a sterile bandage that facilitates clotting, and some Vaseline premixed with adrenaline, because it constricts blood vessels.

During a fight, I'm usually the first to spot a cut. I warn the trainer and ringside doctor that I will be going in. When I can get to the fighter, I wipe the cut with a clean, wet towel to see how deep it is. Whatever I see, though, I stay composed; no one can tell if I'm thinking, *Man, that's a long-ass cut.* That's important, actually, because you'd be surprised how many fighters panic. Right away, I apply pressure—if the cut is deep, for as long as 10 or 15 seconds—and then I swab it with adrenaline and apply the Qwick-AID. I also wipe off the fighter's body; it's a little thing, but you don't want the judges to be swayed by blood evidence. When the timekeeper gives a 10-second warning, I put the adrenaline-Vaseline on top of the cut. All I can do then is hope I've done a good job. I always know I have, but you still need fate and the fighter to cooperate.

INTERVIEW AN ATHLETE

KEN ROSENTHAL
Broadcast Reporter

Think about the situation first: Is the interview for television or print? Pregame or postgame? In a postgame TV interview, for example, I usually have time for just three questions, and my goal is to get the player to give me the story of the game as he or she sees it. I was the first person to interview José Bautista after he tossed his bat after hitting that game-winning home run in the 2015 playoffs. My first question was about the home run itself, the significance of it. But then I asked, "What was going through your mind with the bat flip; why did you do that?" It was important I put it that way. Because I didn't say, "Hey, did you know you were showing up the other team?" he gave a good answer.

In an interview for print, you generally have more time with the subject, so you can warm them up. It's more relaxed, and that really matters if an athlete doesn't know or trust you. I start by asking about family; everyone loves talking about family. Then I use phrases like "I'm wondering why . . ." or "I'm curious about . . ." to get to the more relevant topics. It's a nonaggressive approach. In the end, you don't have the same status as the person you're interviewing—they make more money, they're more famous—so you have to ingratiate yourself. That means being respectful, but not overly so: If you have a hard question, ask it. You're doing your job.

Athletes respond to professionalism. And preparation. So know your stuff. Know what you want to ask. Whatever the medium, though, avoid yes-or-no questions. You want to ask questions that produce longer answers. Using "how," "why," and "what" helps. I rarely ask "How do you feel?" because it's a question lots of people criticize. Still, there are times I know the answer will be interesting, so I ask it a different way: "What's going through your mind?" or "Who are you thinking about now?" In the end, you just want an athlete to convey something meaningful. Accomplish that and you've done your job.

WHERE TO WATCH . . .

A MOTOCROSS RACE AT THE TRACK

Conventional Wisdom: The triples are where the most action is, with riders going sky-high as they traverse the bumps. Any seat near them delivers thrills.

For Your Consideration: Splurge on a pit pass so you can hang with the riders and soak up their culture. Not to mention, it will help you beat the postrace crowds and avoid the lines of exiting cars.

OFFICIATE A YOUTH GAME

They may be kids, but they take their competitions seriously. Certainly, their ever-hovering parents do. So you need to also. That means no break-in-the-action texting or flirting with the newly divorced hot parent. It also means you should . . .

ALWAYS

☑ **TEACH AS YOU ADJUDICATE.** The point is for the kids to learn, and while coaches do teach skills, they don't always explain the rules.

☑ **ANTICIPATE MISTAKES BY THE KIDS** and, maybe, point out an infraction the first time before you call it.

☑ **ADMIT YOUR MISTAKES—DISCREETLY.** And to the coach only.

☑ **READ THE RULE BOOK OF YOUR LEAGUE.** Everybody at the game will think they know all the rules. But you're the only one who has to. (If for no other reason than to remind everyone else what they don't know.)

☑ **BE RESPECTFUL OF PARENTS.** They're just looking out for their kids—at least the ones who aren't sadly trying to live through them.

☑ **EAT BEFORE THE GAME.** A hangry official is an unfocused official.

NEVER

[✗] FORGET TO MEET WITH COACHES AND MANAGERS on both sides before the game to explain how you plan to call it, and suggest strongly that they forward your message to their charges.

[✗] PLAY FAVORITES—say, because one athlete is less coordinated or much smaller than the others.

[✗] MAKE UP FOR A MISTAKE against one team by favoring it later in the contest.

[✗] BE A LITERALIST. Rules are for keeping order and preventing unfair advantage, so it's okay to turn a bit of a blind eye once in a while to keep things moving, if the former is maintained and the latter hasn't occurred.

[✗] TAKE ANY GUFF FROM PARENTS—or belligerent kids, for that matter. Talk to the relevant coach if someone goes a little too far.

[✗] FORGET TO BRING WATER.

TAPE A BASEBALL BAT

Most metal bats have rubber-covered handles so you can get a better grip on the naturally slippery surface and to offer some cushion against the sting that comes when a ball doesn't hit the barrel's sweet spot. But wooden bats come unadorned, and your hands will thank you for coddling them with a softening tape job. (No, the pros don't tape; but you're not a pro—so don't be a martyr.) Come to think of it, the rubber grip on a metal bat can be a bit too thick to hold comfortably, so you may want to lose it and start over with a thinner cover. Whatever your reason, here's how to go about the task.

1. Clean your instrument. For a wood bat, use a fine-grit sandpaper to remove remnants of old tape and other residue from the handle. You can use solvents on aluminum or composite bats.

2. Pick a tape. Cloth, electrical, grip, or tennis . . . all types of tape are fine. What matters is that the tape absorbs moisture. Sweaty palms lead to loose swings.

3. Draw the line. How high up the handle to tape is a personal choice, for the most part. (Some leagues have restrictions, so check the rules.) Mark the bat with a pen or marker so you don't go too far.

4. Begin taping where the knob meets the shaft and work your way up. Angle the tape at about 45 degrees, but leave a ¼-inch space between the strips (see opposite). Cut the tape when you get to the mark you've made. Press the tape firmly to adhere.

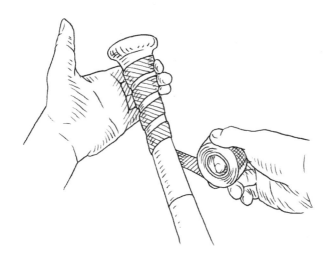

5. Repeat step 4, but this time fill in the empty "lane." Trim any tape that overlaps the knob.

6. Wrap tape a few times around the top and bottom of your grip to seal your edges, pressing firmly each time after snipping.

HOST A SUPER BOWL PARTY

SERI KERTZNER
Cofounder, Little Miss Party

It's tempting to invite everyone you know. Resist that temptation. This is no cocktail party; there won't be any mingling, delicate champagne flute in hand. This is the Super Bowl—all comfort and weekend wear—so invite only as many guests as you can host around the TV without crowding, taking into account kids and the inevitable after-sprawl of beer cans and napkins. Note that where you serve food is just as important as what you serve. Keep it close at hand—that is, near the TV—and grab-and-go style. Think chips and dip, peanuts, pigs in blankets, cake pops, popcorn, wings—minus the heavy sauce. In fact, avoid all saucy foods. It's not worth the mess. And tie a bottle opener to your ice bucket or bin. It will save you and your guests precious moments of searching as the night progresses. To prevent fourth-quarter comas, nix the full bar; beer and bottled water will maintain everyone's stamina. One more thing: If kids do come, separate them from the herd early. Find a corner, stock it with juice boxes, football-themed stickers, and coloring books, and wait for them to conk out around halftime.

WEAR A TEAM JERSEY

DON'T.*

Not if you're older than thirty and not related to the player whose name is on your back. But if you're stubbornly uninfluenced by societal norms of respectability, here are a few tips.

1. *Make sure it fits. (Err in the direction of too big, but not circus-tent big.)*
2. *Old-school (players, design) is always preferred.*
3. *Never put your own name on it, even if you actually played for the team.*
4. *No wrong-color schemes, such as an ironically orange Cincinnati Reds jersey.*
5. *Wear a shirt underneath. (On a related note: No, it's not cute to wear it under your tuxedo shirt at your wedding.)*

THROW A PUNCH

HEATHER HARDY
Boxing Champion

Many people think a strong punch requires a strong arm. It doesn't. What it requires are strong legs and a strong core. Punching is a full-body movement: back foot rotates, followed by hips, followed by shoulder, all causing a weight transfer that translates into punching power (a–b). The arm barely matters. Here's what I tell people: As relaxed as your arm and hand are when you shake hands, that's how they should be when you throw a punch. No tight muscles! The fist is tight, yes, but the biceps and forearm are relaxed, like when you throw a ball. Meanwhile, the front leg should be straight but not locked, and your chin should be tucked. Assuming you are right-handed, your right hand is at your chin and your left hand is at shoulder height, 8 to 10 inches in front of your body. Align yourself with the target: your left arm, elbow, and knuckles and the person you want to hit make a direct line. For a solid one-two combination, jab hard with your left, and as your left comes back, launch the right. Remember: There's no windup with the right. That's a telegraph. You can step forward if you have to, but if you can reach just by extending your arm, that's ideal. Just tighten your core and shoot the right. And while it's true what they say—that you want to picture yourself punching through the target—you want to be sure the punch doesn't pull you forward, because you need to stay balanced so you can defend yourself. So return your right to your chin as fast as you shot it, ready to defend.

SNEAKY SPORTS MOVIES

Rudy or *Miracle*? *Hoosiers* or *Bull Durham*? Few topics stir more pointless debate among fans than the best sports movies of all time. While arguments about the relative greatness of players or teams can at least involve facts (e.g., stats), discussions of cinematic brilliance inevitably devolve into battles of personal opinion. (And that's a waste of everyone's time because obviously the best sports movie ever is *Amazing Grace and Chuck*, which is somehow not one of the three sports movies to win a Best Picture Oscar.*) The wise fan steers clear of such disputes altogether. One way to accomplish that is by turning the question on its head by pointing out that some of the best sports movies are not at first glance sports movies at all.

M*A*S*H

Yes, this 1970 film from director Robert Altman—not to mention the classic sitcom that followed—is a trenchant Vietnam-era commentary on the folly of war (in this case, the Korean). But more than half the flick involves the betting on and playing of a funny and authentic-enough football game between two U.S. Army units. It is quite possibly the most compelling fictional game ever committed to film.

BEN-HUR

Ostensibly a film about a Christ-era Jewish yuppie turned Roman aristocrat, this 1959 classic starring Charlton Heston is actually just one long and reasonably interesting warm-up to the most exciting nine minutes

---

Rocky (1976); *Chariots of Fire* (1981); *Million Dollar Baby* (2004).

in filmdom, a chariot race that plays like a NASCAR–MMA–Burning Man mash-up.

THE GREAT SANTINI

Based on the book by Pat Conroy, this 1979 drama stars the masterful Robert Duvall as a bullying military dad who tries to teach his son how to be a man by humiliating him every chance he gets, including on the basketball court. Anyone who's ever played one-on-one hoops as if it mattered can appreciate the serious sports cred of this emotional gut punch of a film.

BACK TO SCHOOL

Rodney Dangerfield? Check. Robert Downey Jr. and a fictional college that's way more fun than any real one? Check and check. But what makes this 1986 comedy relevant to this discussion is its distinction as the only movie of any genre to make a high-diving competition the apex of its dramatic arc. Triple Lindy? Check!

TEEN WOLF

Michael J. Fox stars in this camp classic about an average American teenager who also happens to be a werewolf. Against all odds, the premise kind of works, but distinguishing this 1985 comedy are two basketball scenes in which our hero loses his temper and gains the athletic prowess that is apparently a perk of the lycanthropic life.

MAKE A TRICK SHOT IN POOL

It can take years of bending over a billiards table to hone a skill set that impresses onlookers. Who has that kind of time? With much less of a commitment, you can perfect a single shot that produces the same effect. Just make sure you walk away before a real game breaks out.

1. Line up the 1, 2, 3, and 4 balls in a straight line that extends from the left side pocket, with the 1 ball hanging over the pocket's edge and all the balls touching each other.

2. Place the cue ball a few inches off the side rail halfway between the balls and the first diamond on the rail.

3. Lining up at a slight angle behind the cue ball, hit it sharply at the right half of the 2 ball (i.e., where it is touching the 3 ball; see right). *Important*: Your stick should make contact with the cue ball on its bottom right quarter (but close to the center). This will get the cue ball to spin out of the way after making contact with the 2 ball.

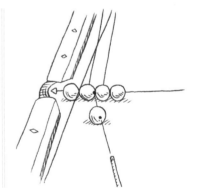

4. Marvel as the 1 ball goes in the left side pocket (a); the 2 ball goes into the far left corner pocket (b); the 3 ball caroms off the far head rail to drop into the near left corner pocket (c); and the 4 ball goes into the right side pocket (d). Well, in theory. It will likely take a few tries to nail this one, but only a few. It really is a simple trick.

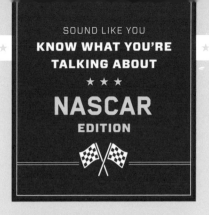

THREE TOPICS UP FOR DISCUSSION

1 WHO'S IN THE DRIVER'S SEAT?

Jeff Gordon has retired. Tony Stewart too. And Jimmie Johnson and Dale Earnhardt Jr. are on the fourth turn of their careers. The good news is that an unprecedented crop of young talent is maneuvering to pass them. The question is whether any of them has the flash or fire to keep the public watching.

2 THE THRILL OF THE CHASE

NASCAR's postseason—a ten-race playoff—debuted in 2004 and has been tweaked a few times since. Most recently, rule changes allowed every race winner to compete for the season championship and instituted a periodic elimination of drivers throughout the ten-race series to keep things interesting. Longtime fans—and drivers—are unconvinced.

3 LONGER ISN'T BETTER

Stock car racing has a bootlegger's soul—its earliest practitioners having embraced speed as a means to outrun the law—but many of the original venues instead featured a sense of stalking with short ovals that promoted bumper-to-bumper pursuit if not all-out speed. The newer "cookie-cutter" tracks are much longer so cars go faster, but the races are less exciting.

WHAT TO SAY WHEN . . .

. . . TWO DRIVERS KEEP "BUMPING" EACH OTHER:
"Rubbing is racing!"

. . . SOMEONE SUGGESTS A WAY TO FIX THE CHASE:
"Maybe they should fix it by not trying to fix it every three months."

. . . SOMEONE COMPLAINS ABOUT A DRIVER THANKING SPONSORS FOR THE TWELFTH TIME:
"Don't worry, he's halfway to his quota."

FOUR TRACKS THAT MATTER

1 DAYTONA INTERNATIONAL SPEEDWAY
The Florida home of the season-opening 500-miler known as NASCAR's Super Bowl remains the high temple of stock car racing. When people complain about boring longer tracks, this one gets a pass.

2 TALLADEGA SUPERSPEEDWAY
As does this one. Come to Alabama for the fastest track times, stay for the party-central infield and the International Motorsports Hall of Fame.

3 HOMESTEAD-MIAMI SPEEDWAY
The Chase is designed to come down to the final race, and here is where that race is. The track may be a bit generic, but the action is most assuredly not.

4 WATKINS GLEN INTERNATIONAL
A road course, as opposed to a stadium oval, has many more turns that demand more moments of deceleration and acceleration and make it quite a different viewing experience. There are two road courses on the circuit. This one is the more photogenic.

Continued . . .

WHEN IN DOUBT, BRING UP . . .

RICHARD PETTY

His seven titles and two hundred victories (earned in the 1960s and '70s) make him the cream of the crop. He (along with his trademark mustache and cowboy hat) is still persona very much grata around the track today.

SAMPLE CHATTER:
"They don't call Richard Petty 'the King' for nothing."

ONE DEBATE YOU CAN WIN

Are racecar drivers athletes?

THE PREMISE

Sure they're brave, but there are those who suggest it doesn't take much skill or talent to sit in a car and drive around in circles.

YOUR POSITION
Damn right they are!

YOUR ARGUMENT

It's no coincidence that many modern-era drivers say they won more races once they started working out. In addition to focusing powers beyond those required in any other sport—with consequences more calamitous if they're lacking—racecar drivers require above-average upper body strength (to maneuver multiton machines), reflexes (to respond to the lightning-quick maneuvers of other multiton machines), stamina (to sit for hours . . .), and conditioning (. . . in high heat). They need to be world-class athletes.

DEFINITELY!

In an attempt to regain market share, NASCAR will schedule midweek races to remove itself from sports weekend pileups.

POSSIBLY . . .

Restrictor plates will be removed and speeds will rise again on the super-speedways, with calamitous results—reminding people why they were mandated in the first place.

WHY NOT?

Driverless cars will spell the end of NASCAR as we know it.

Fun Fact to Impress Your Friends

Early on, stock car owners were permitted to wedge extra gas tanks wherever they could find room inside the chassis, in order to cut down on pit stops. It took almost twenty years, and too many on-track fires, for the keepers of the circuit to realize this wasn't such a good idea. The driver in the fatal crash that finally swayed them: Glenn Roberts, he of the unfortunate nickname Fireball.

SINK A FREE THROW

ELENA DELLE DONNE
WNBA Forward

The biggest mistake people make is putting too much motion in their shot. They'll pop their arm back to launch the ball, almost like a shot put. Or they'll jump, which is a no-no. Kids have to do that, but once you're strong enough, no jumping! Simplicity is the key. The more movement in the shot, the more that can go wrong. And that applies to every step of the process, including the pre-shot routine.

You need to be consistent every time you step to the foul line; routine breeds confidence. A lot of players have different routines, with lots of crazy stuff, but I prefer something simple that can't go wrong: I step to the line and put my right foot just behind the nail in the center. Sometimes there's just a dot. Then I take three dribbles as I look at the floor. After the third dribble, I raise my head and stare at the front of the rim, and I don't take my eyes off it again. Now it's time to shoot.

With my right arm forming an L—elbow at a 90-degree angle—I bend my hand back as it grips the ball. My pointer finger sits straight in the middle of the ball, ideally on the air hole. Meanwhile, my left hand rests on the side of the ball, fingers comfortably spread out. Your palms should never really touch the ball. You want the ball only on your fingers and the pads of your hands—the area just below your fingers and just above your wrist. Right before I shoot each time, I tell myself it's going in. Positive reinforcement is huge. As I begin the shooting motion, I do an ankle pop. That is, I bend my knees a little and flex both ankles so I'm up on my toes. At the same time, from that resting L position, I lift my arm an inch or two up and back—just enough to build momentum to flick my wrist. A flick should provide all the power you need, if you follow through fully. A good follow-through has your fingers pointing to the floor when it is completed. And that's it. Well, except for practice, which is a huge piece of the puzzle. We shoot free throws every day in practice. But I also use them to recuperate between workouts; instead of sitting down, I shoot. As I recover, I'm also working on something crucial to my game.

A BASKETBALL GAME AT THE ARENA

Conventional Wisdom: Sit at center court, six to ten rows above the floor. Among the major sports, you can't find a better mix of overall view and up-close taste.

For Your Consideration: Sit behind one of the baskets, as far down as possible, to witness the surprising quickness of the passes in the lane and the harsh violence under the boards.

JUMP HIGHER

HANS STRAUB
Director of Olympic Sports Performance, Stanford University

Improving your vertical doesn't start with technique; it starts with a sturdy physical base. So work out. Most athletes make significant progress after six to eight weeks of serious lower-body strengthening: squats, lunges, leg lifts, things like that. You'll want to continue building that muscle over time, but after a couple of months you can add some simple techniques to specifically target jumping ability. Chief among them is something called counter-movement, which conditions and trains leg muscles to tolerate the force of jumping in uncontrolled situations, such as going after a rebound. Here's how to do that: (a) Reach for the sky as you balance on the balls of your feet; (b–c) pull your hands down fast as you bend your knees to 30- to 50-degree flexion, making sure to keep your heels off the ground; jump immediately after you hit the prescribed knee-bend depth (d). There is no magic number of reps to recommend. But for power training, less is more, so I usually suggest in the range of eighteen to twenty-four reps, with one to three jumps per rep. This isn't the only technique to use for this purpose—and it's awkward— but it's one of the better ones because it will be useful in all kinds of sports.

a

b

c

d

TAPE AN ANKLE

Whether you were born with weak ankles (Thanks, Dad!) or are nursing a strained one, providing your joints with some additional support is a wise way to go. But not everyone has a trainer on retainer, so . . .

1. Clean and dry the skin, from foot to lower leg. (If you're really serious about preventing infection or irritation, shave the area too.)

2. Present the ankle and foot at a 90-degree angle, and maintain the L shape throughout.

3. Starting at the front of the foot, just below the toes, start to wind pre-wrap (a gauzy bandage you can get at a drugstore) toward the ankle, then up until you reach the bottom of the calf. This will protect the skin from the irritating effects of the tape's adhesive. If you choose to use two layers of pre-wrap, wrap the second layer in the opposite direction—from the back of the calf to the front of the foot.

4. When you're done, cut the pre-wrap from the spool, then press on the loose end to secure it. Remember: You may be applying pressure around a sore ankle, so be gentle.

5. Using 1½-inch athletic tape, wind around the edges of the pre-wrap, at the foot and the calf, to anchor it. Here and throughout, move deliberately to avoid any wrinkles or ripples in the tape.

6. Attach tape to the anchor strip at your calf, then run it down the side of the leg, under the heel, and back up to the other side, making a loop from the outside of the leg to the inside; cut the tape. This "stirrup" provides support to the bottom of the heel.

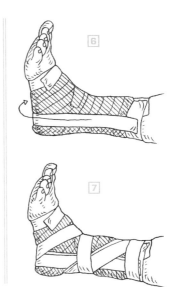

7. Beginning at the back of the ankle, make a forward circuit with the tape to cover most of the ankle bone. Do not connect the ends; cut the tape. This "horseshoe" provides medial-lateral stability without overcompression.

8. Repeat the stirrup and horseshoe steps three times, alternating them to create a rising, overlapping "weave." Each new strip should cover about half of the preceding one.

> *Note: Do not wrap too tightly. Compression is an effective treatment for certain injuries, but it's not the point of ankle taping. Rather, you are providing stability to prevent further injury.*

NAME A HORSE

It's a free country; you should be able to call your Thoroughbred foal pretty much whatever you please. Alas, no. One need only peruse Section V, Rule 6, of *The American Stud Book Principal Rules and Requirements* to encounter seventeen (!) naming restrictions for horses targeted to race or breed. And those don't include the generally reasonable stipulation that names already in the Jockey Club Registry cannot be repeated unless they are both more than ten years old and unused over the preceding five years by raced or bred horses. (Names of horses that were never raced or bred are up for grabs five years after the poor animal's reported date of death.) As it happens, the annual demand—approximately 20,000 names, bestowed in the second year of the animal's life—is met, in part, by those cycling out of the Registry's stable of 250,000 or so previously used monikers. In any event, folks considering what to call their budding Triple Crown winner may not, among other taboos, choose a name that meets the following criteria.

NAMES MUSTN'T . . .

[×] Be longer than eighteen letters or made up entirely of initials, such as JFK or RSVP.

[×] End in "filly," "colt," "stud," "mare," "stallion," or other equine-related terminology; or a numerical designation such as "3rd" or "21st," spelled out or not.

[×] Include only numbers (unless they are names above thirty, as long as they are spelled out).

☒ Reference a living or deceased person unless approval is granted by the Jockey Club (after a written request and explanation).

☒ Have a clear commercial, artistic, or creative relevance.

☒ Be the same as a winner of the Kentucky Derby, Preakness, Belmont Stakes, the Jockey Club Gold Cup, the Breeders' Cup Turf, or the Breeders' Cup Classic; or the same as a winner of any other Grade One stakes race from the previous twenty-five years.

BUILD A BETTER
BUCKET LIST

Sure, you want to see the Olympic 100-meter finals from the stands of some exotic locale. And any fan who doesn't aspire to losing a little hearing at the Daytona 500 maybe isn't such a fan. But if sports is as much about personal fulfillment as it is about one-upmanship, your bucket list has to include some deeper-level check-offs.

YOU MUST GO HERE	BUT DON'T FORGET TO GO HERE TOO	BECAUSE . . .
Kentucky Derby *Louisville, Kentucky*	Saratoga summer meet *Saratoga Springs, New York*	. . . if the Derby is the greatest two minutes in sports, comparable competition and tradition make Saratoga the greatest month. Way prettier track too.
Super Bowl *Location varies*	Division III Football National Championship Game *Salem, Virginia*	. . . with small school teams composed of nonscholarship athletes fighting for a title, it's the purest form of what has become a problematic game.
Indianapolis 500 *Speedway, Indiana*	Grand Prix of Long Beach *Long Beach, California*	. . . it's the closest this country has to an old-school street race.

YOU MUST GO HERE	BUT DON'T FORGET TO GO HERE TOO	BECAUSE . . .
Daytona 500 *Daytona Beach, Florida*	Southern 500 *Darlington, South Carolina*	. . . classic paint schemes, racing legends, and 1970s rock bands make this NASCAR's throwback weekend.
The Masters *Augusta, Georgia*	Q-School Finals *Location varies*	. . . this is really golf's ultimate pressure cooker, with competitors who have paid to audition for the right to try to make a living on the PGA, LPGA, and European tours.
X Games *Location varies*	National Finals Rodeo *Las Vegas, Nevada*	. . . long before there was skateboard culture, there was cowboy culture, and it's on full display here, along with the best ropers, riders, and busters in the land.
Major League Baseball and/ or Little League World Series *Locations vary*	College World Series *Omaha, Nebraska*	. . . it's high-level competition on a relatable scale: better fundamentals than the kids can muster but more heart than the adults can pretend.
Olympics *Location varies*	Olympic Trials *Locations vary*	. . . although there's as much drama—whatever the sport— as at the Games themselves, the ticket price and travel arrangements are far more manageable.

ACKNOWLEDGMENTS

WE CONTINUE TO marvel at our luck for having stumbled into a partnership with Artisan. Every aspect of book publishing—editing (Shoshana Gutmajer, Bridget Monroe Itkin), design (Paul Kepple, Max Vandenberg, Michelle Ishay-Cohen, Renata Di Biase), production (Sibylle Kazeroid, Nancy Murray), and publicity (Allison McGeehon)—is executed with a level of care and respect matched only by the professionalism and excellence of all involved. This well-intentioned, highly functional operation is headed by Lia Ronnen, which figures.

We're also grateful to our illustrator, Peter James Field, whose work added a beautiful layer of understanding to this endeavor.

Jane Dystel, our agent, never disappoints. She's as good as everyone in the business says she is.

Dozens of professional athletes contributed their time and knowledge to the making of this book, for no compensation. We have found that most of the men and women who make their living on fields of play are more than enthusiastic to share their expertise, and we are ever thankful for their generosity.

We are especially grateful to the crew at (and friends of) Elland Road Partners, our content and editorial consultancy, through which we undertook this project. Our roster of reporters, writers, and researchers includes Brendan O'Connor, Charles Curtis, Andy and Brian ("The Brothers") Kamenetzky, Craig Winston, Deanna Cioppa, Anna Katherine Clemmons, Elizabeth Carp, Haylin Belay, Isabella Issa, Justine, Morris, Ryan McGee, Samuel Franklin Tasch, and Jordan Brenner. The making of this book was a team effort. We are fortunate to work with so many all-stars.

INDEX